The APC

The APC

Your Practical Guide to Success

JOHN WILKINSON
FRICS DIP RATING

RICS BOOKS

Material has been reproduced by kind permission of the RICS.

Published by RICS Business Services Limited
a wholly owned subsidiary of
The Royal Institution of Chartered Surveyors
under the RICS Books imprint
Surveyor Court
Westwood Business Park
Coventry CV4 8JE
UK

ISBN 1 84219 037 7

Typeset in Great Britain by Wyvern 21 Ltd., Bristol
Printed in Great Britain by J. W. Arrowsmith Ltd., Bristol

Contents

Foreword   **viii**

Preface   **ix**

1 An overview of the APC   **1**

Official guidance   1

What is the APC?   2

Key concepts and documents   4

      Competent to practise   4

      Competent to practise: streamlining the final assessment   4

      A competency   5

      Structured training   5

      Diary   6

      Log book   6

      Record of progress   6

      Professional development   6

      Change of employer   7

Important dates and deadlines   7

      Enrolment   7

      Acknowledgement by the RICS   8

      Three-monthly reviews by your supervisor   8

      Six-monthly reviews by your counsellor   8

      Interim assessment   9

      Final assessment   9

      Results   9

      Appeals   9

Contents

Finding help   9
Choosing a prospective employer   10
Summary   13

2 The training period   15

The competencies   15
    The common competencies   18
Professional development   19
Structured training   21
    Structured training agreement   23
    Competency achievement planner   24
Summary   26

3 Information management   28

Why keep records?   28
The records   28
    Diary   29
    Log book   31
    Professional development   31
    Record of progress   32
    Progress reports   33
Interim assessment   35
Summary   37

4 Preparation for the final assessment   38

The paperwork   38
The final assessment interview   40
    The objective   41
    The criteria   41
    Competencies   43
The final assessment record   48
The critical analysis   49
    Key issues   50

Options and reasons for rejecting solutions 51
Your proposed solution 51
Critical appraisal and reflective analysis of experience
gained 52
Report writing 52
Summary 55

5 The interview and presentation **56**

Overview 56
The role of the chairman 57
Your role 60
The structure 61
The presentation 62
Questioning technique 65
Interviewee technique 68
Note taking 70
Equal opportunities 71
Conduct, best practice and customer care 71
Summary 73

6 Appraisal, referral and the appeal system **75**

Candidate appraisal 75
Drawing the six components together – the holistic view 77
Role of the chairman 77
The final decision 79
Referral reports 79
Appeals 81
The appeal system 82
Seeking advice and further guidance 82
Summary 83

Conclusion **84**

Index **87**

Foreword

As Head of the Practice Qualifications Department of RICS I have read this book with a great deal of interest. I believe that it is a useful guide for candidates undertaking their APC and complements the official guidance produced by RICS. It will also be a useful resource for employers, supervisors and counsellors of APC candidates.

The author, John Wilkinson has been involved with the APC for over 10 years and is a member of both the Practice Qualifications Group and the Education and Membership Committee of RICS. John has been instrumental in many of the changes that have taken place to the APC and his desire to simplify the procedures and improve the process has been a great help to candidates. His detailed knowledge and experience of the APC make him the ideal person to write this practical and readable book.

I commend the advice provided in *The APC: Your Practical Guide to Success*. However, as John points out in the preface, the APC is constantly changing. Therefore, make sure you follow the most up-to-date guidance provided by RICS and regularly visit the relevant section of the website **www.ricsonline.org**. This way, you will be well on your way to success.

Winifred Cooksey
Head of Practice Qualifications, RICS

Preface

In writing this book my idea was to put my experiences of the last 10 years on paper. The aim and objective being to give you the correct focus and direction at the beginning of the training period, to explain the basic philosophies behind the APC (in particular the competencies) and also to guide and steer you through the training period and the final assessment interview. That's what it is. What it is not is a quick fix to be used the night before the final assessment. There is no short cut to a properly structured training period. My belief is that it is this element which is the key to success and so far as passing the APC is concerned, this is as close as you will come to a guarantee.

I am very firmly of the opinion that the APC is first and foremost a period of training and practical experience. If this aspect of the process is correctly put in place at the outset and performed to the standards required the final assessment should be a formality.

A fundamental aspect of the APC is that from 1 January 1997 the concept of competencies was introduced. From that date the structure and format of the APC began to change very radically. These changes affect the training period, the final assessment interview and the administrative and procedural aspects of the process. It is therefore of vital importance that you fully understand the concept of competencies. These aspects of the APC will be covered in detail in the chapters that follow.

It is important that you understand that the APC is organic, i.e. it is growing and changing. The world does not stand still and this fact was recognized in the Royal Institution of Chartered Surveyor's Agenda for Change which was launched in the summer of 2000. The drive to raise the profile of surveyors and deliver better services globally has led to the recognition of the need for high standards of professionalism. All aspects of the RICS' business activities are being very rigorously reappraised. Demands on surveyors in respect of the services provided is ever increasing, and this in turn leads to the constant review of entry requirements into the profession so that high standards can be maintained – hence the organic and, dare I say, dynamic nature of the APC. It is vital that the RICS invests in the correct 'seed-corn' for the future. Therefore, it is necessary to keep the APC constantly under review so that the process, format and standards are constantly and rigorously reviewed and maintained. This philosophy also applies to entry standards generally and in terms of education a useful reference is Barry Gilbertson's article in *Chartered Surveyor Monthly* (CSM) entitled 'RICS develops programme to deliver status and focus' (September 2000, pp12-13). In this article, Gilbertson refers to a more dynamic approach to maintaining education standards which will involve a 'tougher APC' – so I hope that you will read on and read well.

I remember reading some questionnaires that had been returned by candidates after the spring 2000 assessments. One candidate commented, 'My main complaint is the endless changes to the APC procedure introduced every year'. I do hope that I have helped you to understand why this is necessary.

It is also useful for you to be aware of how changes to the APC take place. The RICS is a membership organization and so decisions involving change are generally made by members, sitting on the various committees that have been set up, under the advisement of RICS staff. So far as the APC is concerned, the committee that sits at the centre of this process is the Practice Qualification Group. Any policy changes to the APC affecting the structure are then approved by the Education and Membership Committee, with changes to the competencies being approved by the appropriate faculty board. The Practice Qualification Group is made up of around 10 people who represent a broad spectrum of the membership and comprises an international dimension, experts across the various faculties, an APC doctor, an employees' representative, a regional training adviser, a Junior Organization representative, etc. There are also, in addition to the members who meet regularly, 10 corresponding members who advise the group on a variety of areas such as the Assessment of Technical Competence (ATC), the European Society of Chartered Surveyors and Australasia. Those far away and exotic places are mentioned in the context of liberty taken as a writer and it would not be fair to exclude from mention my colleagues and some close friends in Northern Ireland and Scotland.

I would like to highlight the excellent work that is being carried out at the moment by the Practice Qualifications Department of the RICS. As the RICS expands globally so must the APC. The APC is indeed going global and is being set up in many countries in Europe including Belgium, France, Germany, the Netherlands, Greece, Hungary and Cyprus. It is also being established further afield in Australia, Singapore and China. This globalization obviously adds to the drive for change and whilst I do have sympathy with the candidate who was frustrated by 'the endless changes', you need to think of these developments in terms of the prospects and opportunities that are opening up for you in your current and future job opportunities around the world in the years ahead!

One final comment. All current matters and developments regarding the APC are published on the RICS website (www.ricsonline.org). Hard copies of this information can also be obtained from the RICS (contact the Practice Qualifications Department on 020 7222 7000).

An overview of the APC

This chapter provides an overview of the basic philosophies, key concepts and various guides and forms that need to be completed, together with the essential dates and deadlines at key stages within the training period. It outlines the roles and responsibilities of some of the key players essential to your training and development such as the RICS, regional training advisers, APC doctors and your employer.

OFFICIAL GUIDANCE

This book will not replicate the official RICS guides to the APC of which there are two: *Candidates and Employers Guide* and *APC Requirements and Competencies*. I suggest that you read this book first and then the two guides. However, it is essential that you do read and study these guides. I still come across too many candidates who have not read them, particularly the *Candidates and Employers Guide*. This fact is made quite obvious to me by some of the questions that I am asked such as, 'Why do I need to know anything about the Rules of Conduct, I have no direct experience or involvement?', 'How long after the final assessment will I receive my results?' and 'What if I am referred, what happens to my critical analysis?' – all of these issues are covered in the guide so beware!

At the time of publication the *Candidates and Employers Guide* and *APC Requirements and Competencies* are being updated. One of the main reasons for updating the guides is the introduction of faculties. The various routes referred to in the *APC Requirements and Competencies* are now linked to faculties and specialisms. These changes are incorporated in this book.

WHAT IS THE APC?

Let's start with the basic philosophies: what is the APC? Quite simply **the APC is the process by which the RICS seeks to be satisfied that candidates who wish to become members of the Institution are competent to practise as chartered surveyors.** To demonstrate this competence, you will undergo a rigorous and demanding period of structured training over a minimum period of 24 calendar months in which you must undertake a minimum of 400 days of relevant experience. The objective is to show that the knowledge of theory gained primarily in further education has been complemented with practical experience. The second part of the process is the final assessment interview.

The APC therefore comprises two components:

1   a period of structured training: during this period you should keep a record of the experience gained in a diary. You must also keep a log book and a record of progress. The log book is a summary of the experience contained in the diary grouped together under the various competencies. The record of progress is the document in which you record your progress of achievement against the various competencies of your chosen route. The training period also incorporates your professional development, an outline of which is given later this chapter and in more detail in chapter 2
2   the final assessment interview: a panel of three practitioners (assessors) will interview you over a period of an hour and form a judgement, or 'assess', whether you are competent to practise as a member of the RICS

The final assessment interview will be dealt with later in the book. The intention here is to look at the key concepts that comprise the training period. However, before doing that I would like to expand and amplify your understanding of what the APC is all about. Think of the APC as the practical training and experience which, when added to the full-time study and learning received at university, leads to membership of the RICS. This concept is illustrated in figure 1.

The illustration in figure 1 is not exactly Einstein, but I hope it conveys my meaning. The first part of the equation can include many variants which will also involve practical experience, for example a degree course at university which contains a sandwich year.

A commonly-held misbelief is that the 'assessment' is all about the questions asked in the final assessment interview. This is not true. The interview panel do not just base their assessment on the questions and answers in the interview, but take into account all other aspects of the two-year period that precedes the interview: the depth and breadth of training; the quality of the documents and written reports (including the critical analysis and professional development record); and your presentation at the interview. All these matters comprise the 'assessment' and at the end of the

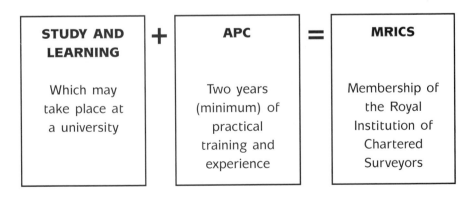

Figure 1 Route to membership of the RICS

interview the panel will view your training and development 'in the round', by taking a holistic view of your performance – and not just the replies to questions in the interview.

KEY CONCEPTS AND DOCUMENTS

Competent to practise

The APC is first and foremost a period of structured training and practical experience which culminates in the final assessment interview, the objective of which is to assess your competence to carry out the work of a qualified surveyor. To be competent is to have the skill or ability to perform a task or function and this ability can vary from being merely able or, at the other extreme, being very expert in any particular sphere of activity. When considering ability or expertise in a task or function, do not think about this concept as only relating to the surveying profession, such as being at the leading edge in a particular aspect of surveying. Changing a flat tyre on a car or preparing an evening meal also demands a level of ability or expertise.

Competent to practise: streamlining the final assessment

In the context of the surveying profession and the APC, the Practice Qualification Group instigated some research in 1999. This was with a view to further defining and clarifying the meaning of 'professional competence' for the purposes of streamlining the decision-making process in the final assessment. This research resulted in the drawing together of the many common, core and optional competencies under five broad headings:

1 knowledge
2 problem solving ability
3 Rules of Conduct and professional ethics
4 business or practice related knowledge and skills
5 personal and inter-personal skills

The idea behind this streamlined approach is to enhance the consistency of the final assessment decision by providing the assessment panel with a clear picture of what competent to practise looks like. In brief, at the final assessment the panel will be looking for you to demonstrate that you meet with the knowledge requirements of your chosen route and that you can also use this knowledge to solve practical problems. You will also have to show that you have developed business skills, an appropriate range of personal and inter-personal skills and that you are aware of and intend to act in accordance with the Rules of Conduct and ethical standards laid down by the RICS.

A competency

A competency is a statement of the skills or abilities required to perform a specific task or function. It is based upon attitudes and behaviours as well as skills and knowledge. For the APC, the requirements and level of attainment for each route are set out in the *APC Requirements and Competencies*. Chapter 2 will develop your understanding of the specific competencies of your chosen route and also how, at the final assessment, these are drawn together by the assessment panel using the streamlined approach referred to above.

Structured training

'Structured training' is, as the title suggests, a more structured approach to the delivery of training over any given period. From 1 October 2000, it is a mandatory requirement for all firms registering new APC candidates to have a structured training agreement in place. In addition, candidates will need to attach a competency achievement planner to their application form, showing the training that has been planned for them.

The structured training agreement and competency achievement planner are simply documents which formalize the intention of the parties to deliver (on the part of the employer) and receive (in respect of the candidate) the training requirements of your chosen route over an agreed period and to specified levels of competence. You will find more details and worked examples of these documents in chapter 2.

You will note that there is no minimum requirement of numbers of training days under each competence other than the overall requirement of the structured training period. This is normally a minimum of 400 days within 24 calendar months.

Diary

The diary is the day-to-day record of how you have been building your experience. The detail contained in it will assist you in completing your log book and record of progress.

Log book

The log book forms a monthly summary of the entries in your diary and is purely a total of the number of days of experience in each of the competencies.

Record of progress

The record of progress charts your progress against the competency requirements of your chosen route. It is a record of attainment which is certified by your supervisor and counsellor. There are a series of forms that need to completed: the three-monthly supervisor's reports; the six-monthly counsellor's reports; the interim and final assessment records and the referred candidates form. These can be found at the back of the *Candidates and Employers Guide*.

Professional development

Another important aspect of the training period is the requirement for you to undertake a minimum of 48 hours of professional development per annum. This will provide you with the opportunity of gaining additional knowledge and skills that might not be available in your day-to-day training and experience. It may be used to complement the requirements of the common competencies. Professional development is recorded in your record of progress and is a simple record of the type and nature of the training, together with the date of the event and the number of hours.

In the context of life-long learning, your professional development never ends. When you have completed your professional development for APC purposes, the RICS then requires you, as a member, to undertake a minimum number of hours of Continuing Professional Development (CPD) thereafter. The concept of professional development is explored in more detail in chapter 2.

Change of employer

If you change employer during the training period, your records will be continued in the usual way but there must be a very clear indication to show the change of employer. In particular, the new position regarding your supervisor and/or counsellor must be indicated for the purposes of certification at the final assessment. The RICS must also be advised of the change of employer. (To do this you must complete and return the change of employer form to the RICS Membership Department. This form will be sent to you when you enrol on the APC.)

Having considered the basic philosophies and some of the documents of the APC, I now want to move on and take a brief look at some of the important dates and deadlines that you will need to adhere to during the training period.

IMPORTANT DATES AND DEADLINES

Enrolment

Enrolment can take place at any time by approaching the RICS for an application pack. However, it is important to note that you cannot backdate the recording of experience. You can only begin recording experience from the date your completed application form is received by the RICS.

Once you have approached the RICS you will be sent an application pack which will contain the *Candidates and Employers Guide*, *APC Requirements and Competencies*, an application form and a disk containing the various templates shown at the back of the *Candidates and Employers Guide*. The disk also contains guidance on the development of a structured training agreement. This does not need to be sent to the RICS but should be kept by your employer and be made available on request to your regional training adviser. However, your competency achievement planner, which summarizes the training proposed by your employer, must accompany your application form.

Acknowledgement by the RICS

Acknowledgement by the RICS will normally take place within two weeks of your application being received. You will also be given a date for your expected final assessment, a form to be completed and returned should you change employer and a copy of the Rules of Conduct.

Three-monthly reviews by your supervisor

Every three months your supervisor will discuss and review your progress against the competencies and complete a progress report.

Six-monthly reviews by your counsellor

At six-monthly intervals your counsellor will discuss and review your progress against the competencies and complete a progress report. This report is a second opinion to the supervisor and will be done in conjunction with you and your supervisor.

Interim assessment

The interim assessment must be completed within one month of the first 12 months of training. The format is outlined in the *Candidates and Employers Guide*. It is important to note that a minimum of a further 12 months training must be completed before you can sit the final assessment.

Final assessment

The final assessment application pack will be sent to you by the RICS approximately five months before the final assessment dates (assessments are held twice a year). You will need to send in the completed application form during the dates specified in the application pack. You will then have approximately one month to submit the required documents for the final assessment presentation and interview. Templates of these documents can be found at the back of the *Candidates and Employers Guide* under the heading 'Candidates Checklist of Important Dates'.

Results

Results will be posted within 21 days of the interview date.

Appeals

An appeal should be received by the RICS no later than 14 days from the date your result was posted.

FINDING HELP

There may be occasions during your training and in the run up to the final assessment when you need help in the form of advice or guidance, over and above that given by your employer. There are a variety of sources that you may approach:

■ APC helpline: the RICS provides a helpline on all aspects of the APC, from start to finish and beyond (Tel: 020 7334 3886)

- APC doctors: the APC doctor scheme is available to you locally. APC doctors are often recently qualified members who can advise and guide you through the APC based on their own experience of the APC. Details of APC doctors in your area can be obtained from the RICS
- regional training advisers: early in 1997, with the advent of the competency-based APC, the RICS set up a national network of regionally-based training advisers. The group comprises a body of members from the faculties, all of whom have surveying, teaching or training experience. The regional training advisers are employed by the RICS and, whilst their principle function is to advise employers on structured training schemes, they are available to advise candidates on all aspects of the APC
- RICS website: the RICS has a website which contains details on the APC (www.ricsonline.org). This is regularly updated and provides a lot of advice and guidance on all aspects of the APC. It is particularly useful for keeping up to date with changes to the APC, but also contains a host of other useful pieces of advice and information that may be of interest to you.

CHOOSING A PROSPECTIVE EMPLOYER

It would not be appropriate for me to close this chapter without reference to the employer. I started the chapter by considering the basic philosophies behind the APC, we looked at the concept of 'competent to practise', and explored the meaning of this in the context of structured training and your progress against the competencies. I believe that this is only one side of the coin. Fundamental to the whole process is the role of the employer and my advice to all candidates is to look before you leap. Before you take up employment don't be afraid to ask a prospective employer what they have to offer in terms of a training scheme.

There is a saying in the North East that 'Shy bairns get nowt', i.e. do not be frightened to ask a prospective employer what it is that they have to offer you by way of a structured training scheme. Questions you should ask include:

- does the employer have a structured training scheme approved by the RICS?
- is there a proven track record of training APC candidates?
- does the employer have its own schemes for providing professional development?
- does the employer have Investor in People? The Investor in People standard is given to firms who set high standards of training and development for staff in terms of commitment to, planning, delivery and evaluation of training
- on a more day-to-day basis, how does the employer plan to assist you in meeting the competency requirements? Can it all be done in-house? Will you be moved between departments or offices? Are secondments/exchanges available with other firms to complement any shortfalls? Also, ask if you can speak to any of the firm's current or recent APC candidates
- who will be your supervisor and counsellor, and what is their experience of the APC?

Patience and understanding is also recommended. Most candidates have an expectation of being ready for the final assessment as soon as the minimum training period of 400 days within 24 calendar months has elapsed. This is not always possible. Sometimes it may be that because of business practicalities or priorities, your employer has not been able to give you the full spread of training against the competencies. Alternatively, you may not have progressed against certain competencies as quickly as expected. Don't forget, we all develop at a different speed in any of life's skills or functions. My advice is to apply for your final assessment when you are ready and you feel confident that you have gained the necessary training and experience, even if that means the training period lasting for 30, or even 36 months. Be prepared to co-operate with your employer and, most importantly, listen to the advice of your supervisor and counsellor.

Remember that your employer does not exist merely to provide APC training for you. There is a business to run and profits to be made. This issue will prove to be a key challenge for most candidates. Whilst you will develop certain expectations concerning your APC training, your employer will also be looking for a return from you by way of hard work, enterprise and fee income! You will need to approach this aspect of the partnership with a degree of understanding and awareness, and give careful thought and consideration as to how you will achieve this balance of the demands of your employer and your own needs to make progress with the APC.

Finally, the importance of the employer cannot be over-emphasized in terms of the appointment of your supervisor and counsellor, both of whom will act as your guide and mentor throughout and, in a lot of instances, probably beyond the training period. The roles will be of vital importance to you throughout the training period and up to and including preparation for the final assessment. It is important that this is an active partnership where the employer takes a proactive approach, by way of interest and involvement, in your training and development.

Over the years I have listened to the debate that the large firms provide the best opportunities for APC training and that small firms may struggle. I cannot agree with this statement. A friend of mine runs a small general practice firm in Carlisle, Cumbria. Over the years he has maintained an interest and indeed a commitment to APC training and regularly employs graduates. From day one there is an active partnership in place, the objective being to ensure the graduate is successful – and indeed they always are! Examples such as this lead me to believe that the APC candidate is often a mirror image of the employer.

So, do not be slow in coming forward, in your own best interest, to find a prospective employer who will provide you with the training and experience that you will need to ensure that success at the final assessment interview is indeed a formality. However, do not loose sight of the fact that you are entering into a partnership and that your employer will also want a return on the investment.

SUMMARY

- It is essential to read the *Candidates and Employers Guide* and *APC Requirements and Competencies*.
- You will need to complete a **minimum** two-year period (400 days within a 24 calendar month minimum) of training and practical experience.
- It is important that you have a clear picture of what is meant by the term 'competent to practise', i.e. knowledge; problem-solving abilities; business and practice skills; personal and inter-personal skills; the Rules of Conduct and professional ethics.
- A structured training agreement must be completed by your employer and you must complete and submit a competency achievement planner to the RICS with your application to enrol.
- Training and practical experience culminates in the final assessment: a one-hour interview with a panel comprising three experienced practitioners who will consider whether you are 'competent to practise'.
- Information and evidence of training and experience must be kept in your diary, log book and record of progress.
- You must undertake a minimum of 48 hours of professional development for every 12 months of training completed.
- If you change your employer the RICS must be notified.
- Experience only counts from the date that your completed application form is received by the RICS. The RICS will advise you of this date.
- Application to enrol must be accompanied by a competency achievement planner.

▓ The interim assessment must be completed within one month of the first 12 months as a further 12 months of training must be completed before you are eligible for the final assessment.

▓ Approximately five months before the final assessment dates you will be sent an application pack by the RICS.

▓ Results of the final assessment interview will be posted within 21 days from the interview date. If you are referred and wish to appeal, this must be done no later than 14 days from the date that your result was posted by the RICS.

▓ Help is available via the RICS, APC doctors and regional training advisers.

▓ When choosing a prospective employer, 'look before you leap' and remember the partnership aspect.

2 The training period

This chapter will look at how to go about managing the training period. It will also develop and expand your understanding of the competencies and how professional development can be used as a tool to assist your progress. In addition structured training will be considered in some detail, with particular regard to the various forms that need to be completed.

THE COMPETENCIES

A key aspect to the successful management of the training period is an in-depth knowledge and understanding of the competencies and the requirements of each RICS faculty or surveying specialism, which I shall refer to as APC routes. It is therefore appropriate that this issue is the first to be considered in this section of the book, as this will get you started on the right track and lead you to success at the final assessment.

In chapter 1 we considered the meaning of the word 'competent' and explored what is meant by a competency. In the broader context the use of competency-based training and, most importantly, competency-based interviewing is fast becoming a world-wide phenomenon. As your career progresses and develops you will find that your appreciation of this subject will grow. However, at this stage it is important that you fully understand competencies in the context of your APC and the guidance that follows is tailored to fit that particular need. Your point of reference is the *APC Requirements and Competencies* which sets out what you need to achieve by way of skills and abilities over the training period. This document can very broadly be divided into two parts. The front part sets out the requirements of each route in terms of specific lists of competencies, with guidelines for the number of competencies to be covered during the training period and also the depth and level of attainment that is required. There is very often a choice of optional competencies and there is also, in most routes, the ability to substitute one of the optional competencies with a competency from the 'full list'. The second part of the document sets out the 'full list' of competencies in alphabetical order and each has a reference, for example Cadastre Ref 005. This reference number is for use on your record of progress.

If you decide to substitute competencies, it should be noted that generally up to one substitution can be made without seeking the approval of the RICS. If you want to make more than one substitution this will require the Institution's approval. You must also be aware that in some routes, for example rural practice, there is often a limit put on the level of competency that may be substituted (often this is at level 2). It is important that you carefully study the *APC Requirements and Competencies* for your chosen route.

The competencies are varied and cover a wide range of technical, professional, business, personal and inter-personal skills and have been written, generally speaking, to three levels which are mainly progressive in terms of skills and abilities. Level 1 comprises the basic understanding of the subject; level 2 adds to the detail; and level 3 is the required limit of knowledge and ability at this stage of your career. Consider the example on page 17 of the building surveying competency of 'building pathology'. This competency progresses in complexity as shown in the example.

Building Pathology

Level 1: To undertake inspections, identify defects and collect information...

Level 2: To diagnose cause and mechanisms of failure...

Level 3: To identify and implement repair methods...

A typical final assessment question may be something along the following lines:

> 'You have been asked to carry out a building survey on a 1960s detached house. In general terms, describe how you would go about the inspection (level 1). Whilst on inspection you notice some lateral cracking to the mortar joints between the brickwork on the gable end, what might be the cause of this cracking? (level 2 – possible wall tie failure) What method of repair would you recommend? (level 3)'

Each route requires you to satisfy three types of competency:

1 common competencies
2 core competencies
3 optional competencies

The common competencies generally relate to personal, inter-personal and business skills and are common to all routes. The core competencies relate to the primary skills of your chosen route. The optional competencies are selected by you.

In deciding at which point you have achieved a particular level of attainment in any of the competencies, there is no minimum number of days. In discussion with your supervisor and counsellor a decision will be made as to when you have reached the required level of skill and ability in any particular competence. The number of days taken to reach the appropriate level will be dependant upon a combination of the following factors:

- your starting point – has there been any previous experience?
- your aptitude and speed of learning in the competency
- the quality of the training and experience given by the employer
- the particular competency – is it measurement or nuclear physics!

A judgement will be made by the supervisor and counsellor who will then sign you off in the appropriate column in the record of progress.

The common competencies

The information set out above relates quite easily to the competency statements of the core and optional competencies. However, I do feel that there are two subtle distinctions between the core/optional competencies and the common competencies that you need to be aware of. The first is that the common competencies are compulsory for all APC candidates. The second difference is that, unlike the core and optional competencies, they are not written in levels. They are simply a series of statements written under seven headings as follows:

1 personal and inter-personal skills
2 business skills
3 data information and information technology
4 professional practice
5 law
6 mapping
7 measurement

The statements under each of the headings vary considerably. They may be very technical and specific such as mapping or, alternatively, be very general in nature, for example under the heading of business skills: 'be familiar with general economic principles'. Some of the statements will be implicit in terms of your training and development and will not need any great or specific application. An example of this is communication skills which develop over a long period of time. On the other hand, some of the requirements will need some formal training, complemented thereafter with work experience to reach the required level of competence, for example quality control and assurance processes.

Structured training will be dealt with later in this chapter. However, my advice regarding common competencies is that when considering your structured training plan, sort out how you propose to achieve the required core and optional competencies and then sift through the list of common competencies. Identify the common competencies where you will receive the appropriate training, implicit within your core and optional competencies. This will leave you with a remainder which will require you to consider additional learning or a specific training course. These actions will qualify for your professional development (which is covered in the next section of this chapter).

The above only deals with the competencies during the training period. I will return to the competencies when we look at the final assessment interview later in the book. At this stage I merely want to put a marker up to say that the final assessment interview is a part competency-based interview for which there are some very specific skills required by both the assessment panel and the interviewee. In a full competency-based interview the panel would not normally question outside your main areas of training and experience. However, in a part competency-based interview some questions may relate to matters of a more general nature. This issue will be covered in more detail in chapter 5.

PROFESSIONAL DEVELOPMENT

For each 12 months of practical training that is completed, you must also undertake an annual minimum of 48 hours of professional development. The idea behind professional development is that it provides the opportunity for you to acquire some of the additional skills and knowledge that it will not always be possible for your employer to provide within the week-to-week business of the practice. This may particularly apply to various common competencies referred to in the previous section of this chapter.

An important aspect of your professional development is that it should be planned and structured in such a way that it remains flexible. It should be designed to complement and support your training and development in the context of the various competencies. Professional development may comprise formal training courses and more informal types of learning such as structured reading, distance-learning programmes and secondments. It is important that you accept ownership of your professional development and you must recognize the planning, acquiring and evaluating of it is your responsibility. Please note that the *Candidates and Employers Guide* also provides excellent guidance on professional development.

A typical annual plan could look like the one presented in figure 2.

On a practical note, make sure that your professional development complements your structured training plan and ensure that at the

---

Professional Development for 2001

Technical skills development: linked to core/optional competencies – normally 16 hours.

Skills development: linked to common competencies – normally 16 hours.

Professional practice skills development: linked to those competencies associated with professional practice, code of ethics and conflicts of interest – a further 16 hours.

Figure 2 Typical annual professional development planner

interim and final assessment you can provide evidence of a planned and systematic approach. There should be a clearly-defined relationship between the topics selected and the competencies. If you feel that there is a need for variation regarding the number of hours allocated, discuss this with your supervisor and counsellor and include an explanation of this departure from the norm in:

■ your interim summary of training and experience as part of your interim assessment (see chapter 3)
■ your final summary of training and experience as part of the final assessment submissions (see chapter 4)

STRUCTURED TRAINING

In chapter 1 we looked very briefly at the concept of structured training which comprises training which is discussed, planned, reviewed and, if necessary, revised, and most importantly forms the basis of an agreement between the parties. This section of the book explores this in more detail.

So far as the APC is concerned, there are two important components to your structured training period:

1   the structured training agreement – setting out the detail of your employer's company policy
2   the competency achievement planner – setting out your plan for the training period in terms of the competencies that you are seeking to achieve, when the appropriate levels of attainment will be reached and how you propose to reach the required level.

Before considering these documents in detail, let us step back for a moment and take a look at some of the mechanics of getting to the stage where your training has actually commenced and the timing of events.

You may be a student who leaves university in the summer and immediately finds employment. To undertake the APC you must approach the RICS requesting an application pack. In response to this initial enquiry, you will receive the application pack from the RICS which will contain the following:

■ *Candidates and Employers Guide*
■ *APC Requirements and Competencies*
■ an application form
■ a disk containing the various templates that you will need to record your training, together with guidance on the development of a structured training agreement

The development of a structured training agreement is mandatory for all candidates and is prepared by your employer. It does not have to be sent to the RICS, but should be kept by your employer and made available on request to your regional training adviser. However the competency achievement planner, which basically summarizes the structured training agreement, must accompany your application form. If it doesn't, you will receive a reply from the RICS putting your enrolment on hold and giving you 20 working days to comply.

If your application and enrolment is acceptable, you will receive a letter from the RICS confirming your application and giving you a date from which you may start recording your experience. Don't forget the importance of this date: before you reach the final assessment you will need to have completed a minimum of 400 days experience within 24 calendar months. This is very important because to be considered for a spring or autumn assessment you must have completed the required minimum training period. It follows, therefore, that a delay of a few weeks in enrolling could put this back six months. Your expected date for the final assessment will be included in this correspondence from the RICS. There is also a reminder as to what you should do if you change employer.

With the acceptance of your enrolment you will also receive a copy of the Rules of Conduct. You are asked to familiarize yourself with the Rules of Conduct as this will form part of your final assessment interview (see chapter 5 for more details).

Structured training agreement

In response to your initial enquiry to enrol, the RICS will send you a document providing guidance on developing a structured training framework. You will probably find that most employers who have recently trained APC candidates will already have a training agreement in place and will be familiar with the RICS requirements. All that will be needed is a degree of tailoring to suit you and your proposed training in relation to time-scales and competencies. However, if this is not the case, the guidance will provide a useful discussion document for you and your employer to plan and agree your training for the next two years.

It should be noted that this document is for guidance only and it may be that your employer may wish to tailor an agreement more suited to their firm. However, the most important aspect is the agreement between you and your employer. The RICS provides a sample agreement and in outline this will contain the following information:

- guidance which refers to the minimum time periods and mandatory records, i.e. diary, log book, record of progress and supervisor's and/or counsellor's progress reports
- a candidate's statement which outlines your commitment, together with a record of the relevant dates from registration to the final assessment
- an employer's statement which outlines their commitment and also provides details of the firm in terms of activities, work areas, staffing levels, geographical location of offices, etc.
- the employer's policies concerning payout of fees, leave

arrangements for APC, professional development and referred
candidates
■ details of the supervisor and counsellor
■ a commitment to all experience being recorded in line with the
guidance set out in the *APC Requirements and Competencies*
■ a diary of relevant dates, particularly showing the three-monthly
reviews with the supervisor and six-monthly reviews with the
counsellor
■ a series of appendices showing useful contacts with employers and
other organizations, the RICS, etc.

Competency achievement planner

As mentioned above, the competency achievement planner sets out
your plan for the training period. There is detailed guidance on
competency achievement planners in the literature accompanying the
Candidates Structured Training Framework. An example of a competency
achievement planner is shown in figure 3.

In keeping with the philosophies outlined earlier in this chapter
regarding the common competencies and professional development,
your development against some of the competencies, for example
business skills, will not have a start and end date. They will continue
throughout the training period and will form the start of your
commitment to life-long learning or CPD.

Your competency achievement planner should be complemented by
one of the following tables which extend and expand upon the
planner:

1 a competencies table which sets out in a more descriptive format
how the competencies are to be achieved in the context of the
type of work to be carried out
2 a monitoring table to be completed for each competency setting
out training completed and training planned

Competency Achievement Planner

Name: Samantha Jackson

Company name: Smith and Co Chartered Surveyors

Ref. no		Qtr 1	Qtr 2	Qtr 3	Qtr 4	Qtr 5	Qtr 6	Qtr 7	Qtr 8
Common competencies									
	Personal & inter-personal skills								
	Business skills								
	Data information and IT								
	Professional practice								
	Law								
	Mapping								
	Measurement								
Core competencies									
00?	Competency 1	Level 1		Level 2			Level 3		
00?	Competency 2	Level 1		Level 2			Level 3		
00?	Competency 3	Level 1		Level 2		Level 3			
00?	Competency 4			Level 1		Level 2		Level 3	
Optional competencies									
00?	Competency A			Level 1		Level 2			
00?	Competency B				Level 1		Level 2		
00?	Competency C				Level 1		Level 2		

Commentary

Figure 3 Example of a competency achievement planner

One of these tables should be used to expand upon the broad detail contained in the competency achievement planner. My preference is for the monitoring table as it allows you to focus on a single competency and provides space to review and progress your training and development. The format of this table also ties in with that of the interim and final assessment format.

This chapter has explained in detail the principle of competencies, including professional development, in the context of structured training, and also the various issues that need to be considered at the beginning of the journey towards the final assessment. The objective is to have an exciting and enjoyable period of travel in which you will learn a lot and set the foundation upon which to build a successful and rewarding career. However, in the final assessment all of the detail and information that comprises the training period will be considered by the assessment panel and used to target questions and lines of enquiry during the interview. It is therefore important that you are aware of how this information will be used at the end of the journey. This will be covered in detail in chapters 4 and 5. However, it is worth pointing out here that in the context of the final assessment it is imperative that you give some thought as to how to manage and record the information during the training period.

SUMMARY

- If you want to substitute optional competencies check the *APC Requirements and Competencies* for your route. You must seek approval from the RICS for more than one substitution.
- Most competencies are written in three levels and are generally progressive in skills and abilities.
- There is no minimum requirement for the numbers of days in each competency. The level of attainment is decided by your supervisor and counsellor in discussion with you.
- Common competencies are compulsory for all candidates. They are not written in levels and comprise a series of statements only.

- The final assessment interview is part competency-based. Some questions may relate to general matters outside of your main areas of training.
- Professional development should be linked to and used to complement your structured training plan. At the final assessment your documentation must show evidence of a planned and systematic approach.
- Structured training comprises training which is discussed, planned and reviewed between the parties to the agreement. There are two main documents:
  1) the structured training agreement
  2) the competency achievement planner

  The competency achievement planner should be complemented by one of the following tables:
  1) a competencies table
  2) a monitoring table
- Do not delay in enrolling. This may put your final assessment back by six months if you miss the key dates.
- All of the various forms and guidance will be provided in hard copy and disk format by the RICS.

Information management

This chapter will look at the various records that you need to keep during the training period. It will provide advice and guidance on how to keep these records and considers their importance in the context of the final assessment. The role of the supervisor and counsellor, particularly regarding the interim assessment will also be covered.

WHY KEEP RECORDS?

You should be aware of the importance of the various records you need to keep in the context of the final assessment. The information contained in your log book, professional development, record of progress and various reports will not only provide the assessment panel with the evidence that you have met with the minimum training requirements, but will also provide a focus upon which to target lines of questioning during the interview. It is therefore vital that you manage and record this information during the training period in an organized and systematic manner as this will greatly assist you in the final assessment interview.

THE RECORDS

Most of the records you need to keep have been considered briefly in outline in the previous chapters. The following guidance pulls all of this together and provides some practical tips and advice.

Diary

A diary must be kept by all candidates and is simply a day-to-day record of your training and experience. The cover page comprises a record of your name, date of registration for APC, route, supervisor and counsellor, and counsellor's declaration confirming that the diary and log book are a true and accurate record of your work. Figure 4 shows a typical format for the diary pages.

Week		
Date	Nature of professional work carried out	Competency reference

(Further details can be found in the templates at the back of the *Candidates and Employers Guide*.)

Figure 4 Typical format for diary pages

With the exception of the Minerals and Environmental Management and Marine Resource Management routes, your diary does not have to be submitted as part of the final assessment documentation. However, it should always be kept up to date and be available for inspection by your regional training adviser on an office visit or by the final assessment panel, if requested. There may be occasions when the assessment panel, through the RICS, may call for your diary to form a more detailed view of your training period.

You can only start recording experience after you have received confirmation of your enrolment from the RICS. The date shown in this acknowledgement from the RICS will be the first entry in your diary. Remember if you change employer this must be clearly marked, perhaps a couple of parallel lines to show a break and a few words of explanation (see figure 5). You must also advise the RICS of this change.

CHANGE OF EMPLOYER	25/9/2000
NEW EMPLOYER	Smith & Co Chartered Surveyors
	35 High Street
	Birmingham
	B1 1AA

Figure 5 Diary entry indicating a change of employer

There are three important pieces of advice regarding your diary:

1 keep it up to date: do not let the weeks slip by without completion. Get into the habit of keeping it up to date on a daily basis. Can you remember how you spent the day, say two days ago? It is likely that you will have forgotten more than you can remember and this is why it is important to record daily
2 get into the habit of using descriptions that relate to the various competencies so that you can make the links to your record of progress and competency achievement planner. For example, 'negotiation and agreement of repair works under a final schedule of dilapidations' will give you all of the links and reminders that you will need to properly complete your other documentation such as the competency table or monitoring table. It will also help you when you are reviewing your overall performance against your competency achievement planner
3 use it as part of the preparation process for the final assessment. It is therefore important that it is well written and clearly presented in order to help you when you are reviewing your training and experience over the two-year period in preparation for the final assessment interview.

Log book

The log book is a summary of the training recorded in your diary on each competency within every 12 months of the training period. Each page will show your name and route and a simple record as shown in figure 6.

Competency title and number	Months												Total number of days
	1	2	3	4	5	6	7	8	9	10	11	12	

Figure 6 Format for the log book

Get into the discipline of completing the log book at regular intervals. This should be at the end of each month and at the end of each 12 months of training as part of the interim assessment. The information is to be sent to the RICS as part of the final assessment submission to be used by the assessment panel.

The log book is a very useful tool for the assessment panel. It provides a very quick and immediate snapshot of your areas of work experience and is used, in conjunction with your record of progress, to structure the final assessment interview in order to obtain the correct balance of questioning relative to your experience.

Professional development

Be proactive in recording your professional development. As explained in chapter 2, there are many aspects of your daily work that count for professional development such as attending meetings, preparing to run a meeting or give a talk, structured reading, etc. Make sure that you are fully aware of what counts and keep a regular record in your diary. This record can then be transferred on a monthly basis to your log book.

Record of progress

The record of progress templates at the back of the *Candidates and Employers Guide* enable you to keep a record of your development against the competencies. These forms consist of the three-monthly supervisor's reports; the six-monthly counsellor's reports; the interim and final assessment records; and the referred candidates form. There is a cover page similar to that of the diary, with the exception of the declarations which are made by the supervisor in addition to the counsellor, confirming that the minimum competency requirements of the APC have been achieved. This declaration is to be completed for the interim and final assessment.

There are two formats for recording progress: one for the common competencies which will simply replicate the statement from the *APC Requirements and Competencies* and provides margins for the supervisor's and counsellor's signatures; the other is specifically designed for the core and optional competencies which starts with a column for the reference number of the particular competency. This reference number may be found in brackets at the end of each competency statement in part two of the *APC Requirements and Competencies*. There is a column for the title of the competency and

Number	Title	Level	Supervisor	Counsellor
69	Valuation	1	*SJ 02/01/01*	*JW 10/01/01*

Figure 7 Typical entry in the record of progress

then margins for the supervisor's and counsellor's signature against each level of attainment. A typical example can be seen in figure 7. What you should be aiming to do is make the record of progress the focal point of your meeting with your supervisor at three-monthly intervals, and your counsellor at six-monthly intervals. You need to be proactive in managing your progress. Therefore in advance of these meetings, prepare a note of how you feel your training is going, how you are developing against the competencies and how far you think you have progressed against the various levels for the core and optional competencies and the statements for the common competencies. You can then compare notes with your supervisor and counsellor.

Progress reports

The role of your supervisor and counsellor is most important throughout the training period. Detailed guidance has been included in the *Candidates and Employers Guide*, in the form of the *Supervisors and Counsellors Guide*. This guide explains the background to competency-based training and includes information and advice on all aspects of the supervisor's and counsellor's role and responsibilities.

I do not intend replicating this guide, however, there are a few key issues worth noting:

- the supervisor is responsible for overseeing your day-to-day work, whereas the counsellor is responsible for managing your training at a strategic level
- ideally they should be different people. However, the role may be combined if, for instance, you are employed by a sole practitioner
- ideally both parties should be chartered surveyors. However, the supervisor may be a member of some other professional institution. If this is the case, the counsellor must be a chartered surveyor
- the supervisor should give guidance, support and encouragement

on a daily basis. At three-monthly intervals he or she should assess your progress against the competencies and complete your progress reports

▪ the counsellor has a similar role and will formally assess your progress on a six-monthly basis and complete the appropriate progress report. In reviewing your overall progress, the counsellor will act as a second opinion to the supervisor

▪ both your supervisor and counsellor have roles and responsibilities in confirming the declarations on the front page of your diary (counsellor only) and record of progress (supervisor and counsellor)

▪ at the interim assessment, which should be completed within one month of the first 12 months of training, your supervisor and counsellor will be responsible for certifying that the diary, log book, record of progress and interim summary of training are true accurate records of your training and experience to date

▪ prior to the final assessment, your supervisor and counsellor must certify that the log book, diary (Minerals and Environmental Management and Marine Resource Management candidates only), final assessment record, record of progress and critical analysis are true and accurate records of your training and experience

You must take a positive approach to the meetings during the training period to discuss progress. Make sure that you agree the times and dates for these meetings and are also prepared to give your input. As explained previously, use the record of progress as the focal point for these meetings. Remember, your final assessment will be based on your performance and competency statements and levels, it is therefore important that your training and experience is geared to achieving this goal. The regular meetings with your supervisor and counsellor will be the ideal opportunity to review progress and forward plan how you will fill any gaps.

It is also worth noting that in the summer of 2000 the RICS introduced a system to monitor the accuracy of supervisor's and counsellor's declarations. Chairmen of assessment panels have been given authority to request that regional training advisers visit employers when doubts have been raised concerning the candidates readiness for the final assessment.

INTERIM ASSESSMENT

Within one month of recording 12 months of training, or the completion of your sandwich placement from the date of enrolment, you should in conjunction with your supervisor and counsellor complete the interim assessment of the training and experience that you have gained up to that date. The date of the interim assessment is important because a further 12 months of training must be completed before you can apply for the final assessment.

This is a very significant juncture of your APC, giving you the opportunity of reviewing progress and forward planning the final 12 months of training.

There are three forms which need to be completed:

1   progress to date: this form is based on the monitoring table which you will have used in conjunction with your competency achievement planner. It requires you to write, in approximately 1000 words, an account of your first 12 months training and experience. There is also a column that allows you to plan your training for the second part of your training period. This may comprise a note of competencies or levels where further experience is needed

2   forward plan: this form requires you to write, again in approximately 1000 words, an explanation of how you will gain the training and experience that is necessary in the second part of the training period. It should be written in conjunction with the competency statements and levels

3   supervisor's and counsellor's report: this form will mainly be

completed by your supervisor and counsellor. It will draw together the information contained in your supervisor's three-monthly reports and your counsellor's six-monthly reports. There is also provision for your comments. The form contains a section for certification by all parties declaring that the interim assessment has been completed and that your diary, log book and record of progress have been correctly completed and maintained

You should also include in the forms some information about your professional development. This should comprise a history of the main elements, together with a summary of the key learning gained from each element of your programme of structured professional development. As explained in chapter 2, do not forget that at both the interim and final assessment the assessors will be looking for clearly-defined links between your professional development and the competencies. There must be evidence of a planned and systematic approach as opposed to an *adhoc* or random selection of professional development topics. For example, if you are training to be a valuation surveyor a two-hour lecture on rocket science would not be an appropriate choice of professional development.

The interim assessment will provide you with an ideal opportunity to sit down with your supervisor and counsellor to review progress and forward plan the remainder of your training period. The layout, content and detail on the various forms will provide the focus for these discussions.

All of these forms can be found at the back of the *Candidates and Employers Guide*. The guide also contains very comprehensive guidance on completing the forms.

It should be noted that the format of interim assessment as described above was introduced in the spring of 2001. The previous system comprised a 3000-word report, outlining the training and experience under each of the competencies. This was submitted to the RICS, together with your diary, log book and record of progress. The report and various documents were then forwarded to an assessor who would provide guidance on the breadth and depth of experience and written communication skills based upon the presentation and content of the 3000-word report.

This approach has now been replaced by the method of self assessment. However, although the forms referred to do not need to be submitted until the final assessment they are still an important part of your pre-assessment submissions. They will therefore form part of the final assessment judgement of the panel. You should also be aware that your regional training adviser may wish to see these documents. Failure to provide evidence that the interim assessment requirements have been completed may result in your final assessment being delayed. Make sure that the interim assessment is completed on time and is readily available.

SUMMARY

- The information and evidence contained in your diary, log book, professional development and record of progress is very important because it will be used in the final assessment to satisfy the panel that you meet the training and experience requirements of the APC.
- The diary must be available for inspection if requested by the regional training adviser or the assessment panel.
- Get into the habit of completing the diary daily and your other records at regular intervals.
- The record of progress comprises a series of forms to show your development against the competencies.
- Be proactive in all meetings with your supervisor and counsellor. Plan and prepare for them.
- In the interim assessment you must provide evidence of a planned and systematic approach to professional development.

Preparation for the final assessment

This chapter will cover the months in the run up to the final assessment interview. It will consider the paperwork that needs to be completed for the final assessment. In order to assist your preparation it will provide detailed guidance on the methodology that will be adopted by the panel during the interview. And finally, advice on preparing the final assessment record and the critical analysis will be given.

THE PAPERWORK

You will recall from chapter 2 that in the letter you receive from the RICS confirming your enrolment, you will also be given a likely date for the final assessment. This date will have been held on record by the RICS and five months before the final assessment dates you will be sent a final assessment application pack. There are two very important points to note:

1 if you do not wish to sit your final assessment on the proposed date, the onus is on you to notify the RICS that you are deferring
2 should you have any special needs or disabilities, the RICS will, subject to notification, take appropriate measures to assist you at the assessment centre. There is a box on the application form that needs to be completed with regards to this

Upon receiving your application pack you will need to send in the completed application form. You will then have approximately one month to complete and send all of the required documents to the RICS. With your application pack you will receive guidance on completing the various forms and a useful checklist comprising a list of the documents that need to be forwarded to the RICS. There is a checklist for candidates applying for the first time and another for candidates who have been previously referred.

You will need to complete part of the front page of the assessment panel's marking sheet with personal details and a passport-sized photograph. You will also have to complete the final assessment application form to provide various personal details, along with information concerning your training and experience. This latter point is very important because it will assist the RICS in putting your final assessment panel together. The RICS will match panels and candidates in terms of background, training and experience so that the detail of the interview may be correctly targeted by assessors with experience in similar areas to yours. The other main form that you will need to complete as part of the application pack concerns your professional education and employment details, outlining your history of education and employment up to the date of the final assessment.

When applying for the final assessment you may not have completed the minimum 24 calendar months of training. You may therefore not have reached the required levels in some of your competencies. If this is the case you will need to complete a declaration stating that at the date of the final assessment you will have reached the required levels. The assessment panel will seek to confirm this on the day of your final assessment.

Don't forget, if you need any help or advice you can contact the RICS.

THE FINAL ASSESSMENT INTERVIEW

This book has been written in a logical order, that is to say in an order which follows the way in which your APC will actually take place. At first sight therefore it may appear to you that consideration of the final assessment interview at this juncture is a little premature. The reason for this is to give you an understanding of competency-based interviewing so that you can start the mental preparation for the interview at an early stage. In particular, it is important that you are focused on this concept in the two to three month run up period whilst you are preparing your critical analysis and presentation.

I would also like to add a personal observation. I have been involved with APC training for a decade and I have not yet met a candidate who has been able to turn up on the day, without any preparation or revision, and be successful. I can only compare the final assessment to training for a major sporting event. To be successful, the athlete will need to approach the run up to the big event in a planned and structured way, looking to peak, in performance terms, on the day. You will need to apply the same approach to the run up to your final assessment. Put the time and the effort in and you will be more likely to succeed rather than just turning out on the day.

In this run up to the big event you need to have a clear understanding of competency-based interviewing so that you have an informed approach to the revision and preparation needed for the final assessment interview.

All good interviews essentially comprise eight important aspects:

1 objective
2 criteria
3 role of the chairman
4 structure
5 questioning technique

6 note taking
7 equal opportunities
8 conduct, best practice and customer care

This chapter will look at the objective and criteria in terms of how they link to competency-based interviewing. I will then deal with the remaining aspects of the interview in chapter 5.

The objective

The objective of any interview must be clearly defined at the outset. Interviews are conducted for a variety of reasons: for employment; promotion; appraisal; or dismissal.

The objective of the APC is to ensure that only those candidates who have an acceptable level of competence in carrying out the work of a professionally qualified surveyor on behalf of a client or an employer are admitted to professional membership of the RICS. This objective is set out in the first part of the *Candidates and Employers Guide* and is simply to test whether you are 'competent to practise' as a chartered surveyor.

Your competence will mainly be judged by the assessment panel asking questions, a lot of which will test your ability to put theory into practice. Throughout the interview the assessors will set questions based on everyday problems faced by practising surveyors. This is a very important concept. The APC is a practical test and assessment panels are made up of practising surveyors who are best placed to test your competence – based on their own up-to-date knowledge and current experience of the problems, issues and difficulties faced by the profession.

The criteria

In any interview situation it is important that criteria have been set. The criteria are the standards or bench-marks against which all candidates are judged. They provide the consistency and uniformity required to create fairness, or equality of opportunity, for all candidates.

For the APC, the criteria are set out in the front of the *Candidates and Employers Guide*. They can divided between the immediate criteria that the panel will expect to see in place on the day, and the developmental criteria which have a longer term connotation. Management is a good example of the latter context. Management skills and abilities, if nurtured and developed, evolve over a period of time, whereas certain aspects of technical training can take place much more immediately.

The immediate criteria that will be tested by the panel are that you:

- have learnt to apply your theoretical knowledge through professional training and experience to attain practical skills
- have achieved a satisfactory level of understanding and application of the skills that form an essential part of the knowledge base of your chosen route
- are aware of the need to pay particular attention to accuracy and essential detail to safeguard the interests of employers and clients
- can communicate effectively – orally, in writing and graphically – and prepare reports which are well structured, grammatical and spelt correctly
- are aware of and intend to act in accordance with the Rules of Conduct; possess the highest level of professional integrity and objectivity; and recognize your duties to clients, employers and the community

With regard to the developmental criteria, you are also expected to demonstrate that you have developed so that you:

- are a good ambassador for your profession, the RICS and your employer

■ are aware of the professional and commercial implications of your work

■ understand your clients' and employer's thinking and objectives

■ have an up-to-date and developing knowledge of legal and technical matters relevant to the work that you do and the law of the region or country in which you practise

■ are able to play a role in a team and build up experience in client contact

■ are aware of the operation of general economic principles

■ have developed the confidence to work unsupervised

■ are able to demonstrate motivation, initiative, and administrative ability

These criteria overarch the whole assessment process. Additional criteria have also been set for the critical analysis and the presentation which I shall deal with next.

You may be feeling somewhat lost at the moment and wondering where all of this is going. What I am now going to do now is pull the objective and criteria together in the context of the competency, or more particularly part competency-based interview. Then in the next chapter I will give lots of examples of how you can demonstrate in the interview that you meet the various criteria.

Competencies

The final assessment comprises a part competency-based interview. The objective of a competency-based interview is to allow you to demonstrate your skills and abilities against the various competencies that form the requirements of the training period. This will be done by the assessors asking questions and setting oral problems which draw on your experience and demonstrate problem-solving abilities, i.e. the ability to put theory into practice. In a criterion-based interview, the interviewer will mainly focus on knowledge and skills, whereas in a competency-based interview he or she will also consider attitude and behaviours.

You should note that the final assessment is a part competency-based as opposed to full competency-based interview. In a full competency-based interview, the interviewer would not question outside of your actual training and experience. However, the objective of the APC is to consider whether you are competent to practise as a chartered surveyor and so the assessors will test knowledge of wider issues, awareness of your limitations and matters of concern to the profession. You will therefore on occasions be stepping outside of your actual training and experience. A classic example of this is the Rules of Conduct. The senior partner or managing director of your firm will usually deal with many aspects of the Rules of Conduct, such as the client account regulations. Therefore in normal circumstances you will not gain hands-on experience of such matters. However, you will still be expected to have some knowledge of the basic issues.

So how will the objective, criteria and competencies be drawn together by the assessment panel during the course of the interview? The answer is quite simple. The panel will take a competency against which they will test a variety of the criteria with a view to deciding the objective of the interview: are you 'competent to practise' as a chartered surveyor? For an example of this see figure 8.

The aim will be to test you over the full range of the criteria during the course of the interview. However, it is not necessary to test all the criteria against every competency. This is because the testing of the ability to put theory into practice criterion will also test a number of others. In the example on page 45, for instance, testing the ability to put theory into practice will also demonstrate knowledge of legal and technical matters, operation of general economic principles, etc. Generally, you will find that whilst testing your ability to put theory into practise, an experienced assessor will draw out details of your knowledge, skills and abilities in relation to a large number of other criteria.

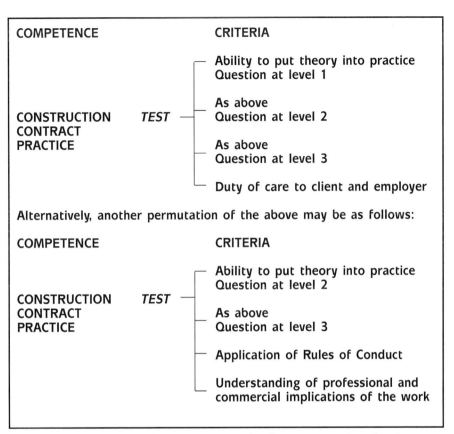

Figure 8 Questioning for competence in the construction faculty (quantity surveying)

An example of the questioning in line with figure 8 may be as follows:

- 'What are the main criteria that you would consider in deciding upon a method of procurement?' – level 1
- 'A client approaches you with a one hectare greenfield site and wants a 5000m² office block building within six months to a basic specification. How might you advise the client?' – level 2

- you may have suggested a design and build contract and the final line of enquiry may relate to the detail of, 'What are some of the main issues that should be included in the form of contract?' – level 3
- you may also be questioned on Professional Indemnity Insurance requirements – Rules of Conduct
- this may be followed by the assessor asking you, 'Outline the quality control and assurance measures that you would put in place to protect your clients interest' – duty of care
- finally, you may be asked for, 'A broad indication of the construction costs per m² relative to your area of practice' – commercial awareness/implications

At the end of the interview, the assessment panel will make a judgement as to whether you have demonstrated the required level of competence. As shown in the example above, the panel will do this by taking any of the appropriate competencies and asking questions to ensure that you meet the criteria that have been set. On this basis you will then be considered for professional membership of the RICS because the objective of the APC has been met.

It is also important to note that in a 60-minute interview, the panel will not be able to test a full two years of training and experience. They will need to be selective, so don't worry if there are gaps and omissions. The panel may have been satisfied by some other piece of evidence, in the written submissions, concerning your competence: it is not all down to questions and answers in the interview.

Having explained the basic concepts of a part competency-based interview, what follows is guidance on how you should build this into your revision and preparation for the final assessment. Going back to the comments made about the occasions when the assessor will step outside of your actual training and experience, shown on page 47 are some examples and explanation of this aspect of the interview.

■ Remember the candidate who told me that he knew nothing about the Rules of Conduct because the senior partner in the firm dealt with these matters? Even in the absence of hands-on experience, the criteria set for the final assessment expects you to have some knowledge of the Rules of Conduct.

■ Consider yourself as a quantity surveyor having only hands-on experience of small works types of contract. This can happen, but you will still need an understanding of other types of contract.

■ Think about politics and economics and the effect that government economic policy can have on interest rates. These in turn can have an effect on all aspects of the property world, the construction industry, etc.

■ Some years ago I observed an interview and felt that an assessor had been hard on a residential property candidate because he had no experience of council tax and a number of questions were asked on this. The assessor's reply was that he could stop someone in the street and would most likely get the answers to the questions asked.

■ On another occasion, I watched a valuation surveyor with no experience in rating being asked some very basic questions. He was a commercial management candidate and the scenario was one of questions being asked by a tenant of a shop about a large rates demand. The assessor's view was that he should know a little about the subject if nothing else, to understand his limitations and advise the tenant where to seek advice.

These examples should give you an understanding of why the final assessment needs to be a part competency-based interview. They should also provide some guidance in terms of the background reading you will need to do in preparation for this. Sometimes when

I am training candidates in preparation for the final assessment, I run a brainstorming exercise. I ask everyone in the group to prepare a list of background preparatory reading for the final assessment and we often fill 6 to 10 pages of a flip chart. It is an exercise that I would strongly recommend that you carry out while planning your preparation and revision.

The remainder of this chapter will consider two other aspects of your preparation and run up to the final assessment: the final summary and critical analysis.

THE FINAL ASSESSMENT RECORD

The format of the final assessment record is very similar to the interim assessment outlined in the previous chapter. However, for this summary you will only use the progress to date and supervisor's and counsellor's report forms. The objective is to give the assessment panel an outline of your training during the 12 months prior to the final assessment. This should be completed in approximately 1000 words. It will be based on your progress against the competencies.

In the progress to date form the column entitled 'training planned' may be used to outline your experience gained in the last three months. The reason for this is that there will normally be a period of three months between submission of the documentation and the final assessment. During this period it may be that you have planned to acquire further training and experience in some of the competencies and this information will assist the panel in forming a complete picture of your training.

The supervisor's and counsellor's report form will draw together the information contained in your supervisor's and counsellor's progress reports for the second twelve months of the training period. It will include your comments and provide space for certification that the final assessment records have been completed and that your diary, log book and record of progress have been correctly completed and maintained during the second part of the training period.

THE CRITICAL ANALYSIS

The critical analysis is a written report comprising 3000 words. It is a detailed analysis of a project with which you have been extensively involved in during the training period, the conclusion to which involves a critical appraisal of the project, together with a reflective analysis of the experience gained.

In recent years the choice of topic for the critical analysis has been the source of much confusion. You may be working for a large firm and have been involved with an instruction or project which is considerable in size or importance. Your role in the instruction or project would be an appropriate topic for the critical analysis (see the further guidance on pages 50 to 51 concerning 'key issues'). On the other hand, the instruction or project may not be too complicated or of great value. It may simply be typical of the type of work with which you are involved during your training period. However, this is an equally suitable topic for the critical analysis.

It must be emphasized that you are not expected to be running the project. It is your involvement or role in the team that you are expected to outline, analyse and provide comment on. Also, it is not necessary that the project has a start and finish. It may be that at the time of writing your critical analysis the instruction or project has not reached a conclusion. Your report will comprise the detail up to the date of writing and it may be that it contains a prognosis of the outcomes. Alternatively, the outcomes may be known at the date of the final assessment and you may wish to include them in your presentation.

The report should be a maximum of 3000 words and should be supported by an appropriate number of appendices. However, it is quality not quantity that is important, so use a word count and do not go over the top with appendices. Appendices should be included to support your report, not to add or expand upon it.

The format of the critical analysis is clearly set out in the *Candidates and Employers Guide* and it is important that this format is followed. One of the main reasons for referral is that this guidance is not followed and the format of the critical analysis becomes similar to the type of report that you would write at work. The main headings of the report should therefore be as follows:

- key issues
- options
- reasons for rejecting certain options
- your proposed solution to the problem/s and reasons for this choice
- critical appraisal of the outcome and reflective analysis of experience gained

The assessors are looking for good communication skills as well, so think about the layout of the report, presentation and use of photographs and plans, grammar, spelling, number of words, index, pagination, etc. Put yourself in the position of a potential client picking the report up for the first time. Would you be impressed with the presentation, the content and the advice? Would you consider awarding the contract?

The assessors are also looking for a high level of professional and technical skills, so make sure that this aspect of your report is checked and double checked.

Now let us consider each of the above headings in turn:

Key issues

The project that you have been involved in could be quite extensive.

If you select too many key issues it is likely that you will merely skim the surface of them and not get down to what is required, i.e. a detailed analysis. So be selective. You may wish to select just the one key issue. It is possible that this key issue may be common across a number of projects with which you have been involved, and this is acceptable. Be careful, if you choose too many key issues you will not hit the level of detail required to call your report a detailed analysis. Try to think about the depth required being about level 3 of the various competencies involved.

Options and reasons for rejecting solutions

It is uncertainty that creates the need for experts, and it is the diversity of solutions to any particular problem that leads clients into needing professional advice. Therefore, before proposing a solution to a client, you will need to consider all of the options. You will need to demonstrate your ability to think laterally and show that you have genuinely considered the options over and above your preferred solution. Give reasons why some solutions may not be feasible. Do not fall into the trap of going down one route only. The guidance in the *Candidates and Employers Guide* clearly requests that you consider options or possible courses of action and also that you give reasons for the rejection of those options not selected.

Your proposed solution

You must give a detailed account of the reasons supporting your adopted course of action, and here again it is important that your thoughts cover a broad canvas. Too many reports just cover the technical aspects of a particular job. Make sure that you paint on that broad canvas. Think about all of the aspects that support your decision: customer care; financial; technical; professional; the Rules of Conduct; ethics; and conflicts of interest.

Critical appraisal and reflective analysis of experience gained

The conclusion to your report must include a critical appraisal of the outcomes, together with your own views and feelings as to what you have learnt from the experience. This part of your report may comprise around a quarter to a third of the total number of words.

The critical appraisal is about being introspective. All good professionals need to be able to look at a project, consider what has gone well, identify what has not gone so well and plan how you might improve upon your actions the next time you carry out a similar task. This will comprise your critical appraisal of your project.

The next step is to stand back from the project and reflect upon what you have learnt from the experience gained.

The assessors will be looking to take your critical appraisal as a starting point to question you beyond what you actually did and to probe your understanding of the wider issues surrounding your project. It is therefore useful to start these processes whilst you are writing your critical analysis, not once you are in the interview.

Sadly, these two aspects of the critical analysis have proved to be the most lacking in recent years. There have been more referrals as a result of these aspects than for any other reason.

The critical analysis is a professional piece of work and should therefore be signed and dated by you. Don't forget your supervisor's and counsellor's certification, as required in the *Candidates and Employers Guide*.

REPORT WRITING

I want to close the chapter by giving you some practical guidance on report writing. With regard to the critical analysis, if you follow the 10-point plan set out below, together with the practical guidance covered earlier, you should be well on the way to success:

1   the objective: never lose sight of it! You are looking to write a detailed analysis of a project (or projects) with which you have been involved during your training period. The conclusion to this report involves a critical appraisal of the outcomes, together with a reflective analysis of the experience gained. Keep this in mind throughout

2   brainstorm the subject: brainstorming is a simple technique where you have a topic or subject and write notes, in no particular order, of all of the thoughts and considerations that come to mind

3   prepare an outline and consider the appendices: start to put your brainstorming into an order, using headings and important issues. Then consider the appendices that will be useful to support or shed light on the critical analysis. Do not fall into the trap of using the appendices to add to the volume of words, it is quality not quantity that the assessors will be looking for

4   consider visual aids, plans and photographs: for simple reasons, photographs can speak a thousand words and you have been set a limit of 3000 words for the text! However, think carefully about the need for and use of the visual aids

5   stand back and review where you have got to: are you still on course to meet your objective? Does everything look interesting and entertaining? How would you view the content if you were on the assessment panel?

6   write it out in full: start pulling the detail together in terms of the text and appendices, plans, photographs, etc.

7   once again review it: look at the number of words, use a word count, and also be particularly careful with spelling and grammar

8   polish it: think of an attractive cover page, an index, binding and paragraph numbering. Make sure that it is signed and dated and certified by your supervisor and counsellor

9   test it for potential areas of questioning: don't forget, the panel
    will be extending their questioning beyond what you actually did
    and will also probe your understanding of any wider issues
    surrounding the project. It might be useful to ask one or two of
    your colleagues in the office to read your critical analysis with a
    view to asking you some questions along these lines

10 the objective: has it been met? Go back to where you started and
    consider the following:

    ■ have the key issues been made clear?
    ■ have you considered the options, and in particular the reasons
      for rejecting certain options/solutions?
    ■ is the proposed solution supported by detailed reasoning?
    ■ does the conclusion include a critical appraisal of the outcome
      and a reflective analysis of the experience gained?

The critical analysis is not an exam and so you will have access to
texts, references and a whole host of technical and professional
references. It is therefore very important that you narrow the key
issues down so that you can write to the appropriate level of detail. In
doing this, take care to ensure that the technical and professional
references are to a high standard as this will be an important issue in
the eyes of the assessment panel. In summary, the criteria that the
assessors will be looking to apply to the critical analysis to decide
whether it should be passed or referred are as follows:

■ have the key issues been identified?
■ have all the options been considered?
■ are the reasons for rejection of certain options clearly stated?
■ is the preferred solution supported by sound judgement?
■ does the conclusion contain a critical appraisal and reflective
  analysis of the experience?
■ has the candidate demonstrated high standards of spelling and
  grammar?
■ does the report contain high standards of technical and
  professional skills?

You will recall that earlier in this chapter the criteria that 'overarch' the final assessment process were considered. The above criteria clearly set out what the assessors will be additionally looking for in the critical analysis.

SUMMARY

■ Approximately five months before the final assessment date you will receive an application pack from the RICS.

■ You must advise the RICS of any special needs or requirements for the final assessment interview.

■ Make sure that you follow the guidance that accompanies the application pack. Remember to use the checklist provided by the RICS.

■ The final assessment interview is part competency-based, so do not loose sight of the wider issues.

■ Always stay clearly focused on the links between the objective of the interview and how the competencies and criteria fit together.

■ The final assessment record is an important document in that it will help the assessors target questions and lines of enquiry. Make sure it is a true and accurate reflection of what you have been doing during the training period.

■ Ensure that the format of your critical analysis complies with the guidelines that have been set by the RICS.

■ Ensure that the context of the critical analysis addresses the key issues and gives reasoned support for your chosen solution or proposal.

■ Make sure that you give proper consideration to the critical appraisal and reflective analysis that is required in the conclusion to your critical analysis.

■ Spelling, grammar, presentation, technical and professional skills are also very important aspects of the critical analysis.

5 The interview and presentation

This chapter will expand and develop your knowledge and awareness of the role of the interviewer and in so doing will develop your technique as an interviewee. The presentation will also be considered in detail.

OVERVIEW

An interview can be described as an information-gathering process in which the interviewer's most important skill is questioning technique. You will do the majority of the talking and the split should be in the ratio of 70:30. At the end of the interview, the assessment panel will consider the information gathered and how well it meets the criteria set for the interview. This in turn will determine whether the objective has been met, which will then determine the outcome: have you been successful?

In chapter 4 we considered the various components of an interview and in particular we considered the objective and the criteria. I now want to move on and look at the other components in more detail:

- role of the chairman
- structure of the interview (including the presentation)
- questioning technique
- note taking
- equal opportunities

■ conduct, best practice and customer care

Under each heading an explanation of how the panel will operate is provided, followed by guidance on how you can improve and enhance your technique with a view to delivering an effective performance, i.e. a performance that persuades the panel that you are 'competent to practise'.

You should appreciate that every interview you face will be different. All firms and organizations will have a slightly different approach and there will be variations in paperwork, time and the format of the actual interview. In the context of the APC, no two assessment panels will operate in the exact same manner. Therefore, the information that follows is provided in the context of guidance only. However, it is hoped that it will be helpful to you.

THE ROLE OF THE CHAIRMAN

The chairman of the assessment panel has a very important role to play during the interview. Let us now look at this role in more detail, particularly regarding the various aspects of the chairman's performance that are aimed at assisting you.

The chairman will have made contact with the other panel members shortly after receiving your detailed information and final submissions from the RICS. He or she will have had a brief discussion with the panel members concerning various aspects of the interview and will normally have arranged to meet them one hour before the first interview.

A critical part of the interview is the opening three to four minutes and during this period the chairman's conduct will be geared towards settling your nerves. The final assessment interview is an 'advanced role play situation'. Consequently, you will probably be more nervous than you would be in a job interview. You could argue that there is much more resting on the outcome of this interview, with many years of effort having gone into the preparation. Therefore, the importance of settling your nerves and 'breaking the ice' is vital.

Figure 9 is a simple stress management graph that explains this concept in more detail.

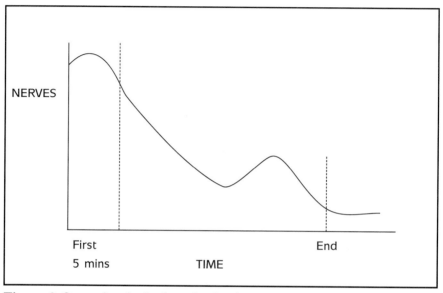

Figure 9 Stress levels during the final assessment interview

At the outset of the interview your nerves will be high. The chairman and panel members will aim to help you settle these nerves. Just before the end of the interview when the chairman will signal the close, your nerves will rise again for one last time. Your nerves may increase somewhat as the interview progresses and you move from one panel member to another.

So how will the panel try to help you settle your nerves? There are a number of things they can do:

■ introductions: as soon as you enter the room, the format will have been agreed beforehand in terms of handshakes, names, and any relevant background information, etc.

▪ structure: the chairman will give a brief outline of the structure of the interview. This will give you an idea of how the panel intend to organize the time and will help you know what happens next

▪ comfort: the panel will make you feel comfortable by offering you a seat, water, jacket off, etc.

▪ notes: the chairman will explain that the panel will be keeping notes. Do not be put off if you see the panel scribbling away furiously, this is done to assist with your assessment at the end of the interview

▪ health check: after you have settled in and before you move on to the presentation, the chairman may check to ensure that you are 'fit and well and ready to proceed' – or similar words to the same effect. This check is to ensure that all candidates are given equality of opportunity. If you feel unwell before the interview it is important that you do not proceed. You should tell the chairman who will advise you what to do

▪ the ice breaker: the opening question asked by the chairman will be designed to 'break the ice'. The only way that you can get rid of nerves in an interview is by talking them out! The chairman will ensure that your first question is easy to answer and may be phrased something along the lines of, 'Tell us in your own words what sort of work you have been involved in over this last six months? Make sure that you are prepared for this question. Practice your response as this will help you at the beginning of the interview when your nerves will be at a peak

▪ last word: the panel will always let you have the last word. The chairman will say something like, 'At the end of the interview I will give you the opportunity to come back on, add to or clarify anything that we have discussed'

The chairman may also provide the following additional support:

- have a word with you outside the room, run through the interview structure briefly and then escort you into the room to meet the panel
- keep you briefed at each stage of events even though the structure was outlined at the outset. This will help you with your nerves and will be designed to give the interview some continuity. The chairman may use phrases such as, 'Thank you for your presentation, we are now going to discuss some aspects of it with you. My colleague ... will begin'

Your role

There are a number of ways that you can help yourself prior to the interview:

- make sure you know where the assessment centre is. Time your journey to give yourself plenty of time. Try not to put pressure on yourself by worrying about these things on the day – sort them out beforehand
- if you have had any problems with the journey or are unwell on the day, let the RICS staff know. This can be taken into account during the interview
- look the part. There is no doubt in my mind that a good first impression will give you a mental boost and will help with your nerves and confidence.
- rehearse your opening lines and prepare for the ice breaker

Figure 10 shows how we let first impressions, which are often formed in the first few seconds of meeting someone, form our views and opinions.

When we meet someone for the first time, our initial impressions will be based on such things as stature, dress, deportment, etc. The person

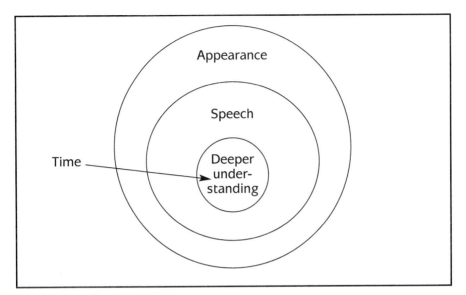

Figure 10 First impressions

will then speak which will add to the mental picture that we are building. We may immediately relate to the person's dress sense or accent, or we might find these do not conform with our 'norms'. We may, therefore, have created a 'barrier' which can affect judgement and may prejudice our views and opinions. It is only when we get beyond these first impressions that we will really get to know someone and develop a deeper understanding of them.

I should point out that the assessment panel will have been trained to deal with first impressions. To counterbalance this they will probably take notes during the interview to ensure that you are judged on your overall performance rather than first impressions.

THE STRUCTURE

A well structured interview has certain advantages. It will:

■ provide order and discipline

■ help the panel cover the agenda – nothing will be missed
■ assist the panel with time keeping
■ provide a focus to proceedings

You will probably find that the interview will start with a brief welcome and settling in period. The chairman will then ask you to give your presentation. This will be followed by approximately 10 minutes of questions on the issues raised. Following this, the panel will move on to consider your wider areas of training and experience in relation to your chosen competencies, with the chairman and assessors taking it in turn to question you. This part of the interview may last for up to 35 minutes. The chairman will then spend a few minutes closing the interview and will give you the opportunity of the last word.

THE PRESENTATION

The presentation will be based on your critical analysis and the objective is to give the panel an outline of the purpose, investigations and conclusions concerning the work detailed in this report. It should last for 10 minutes.

Following the chairman's introduction you will be asked to give your presentation. You will be allowed to sit or stand. The panel will not, in normal circumstances, interrupt you during the 10 minutes, although the chairman may let you know that you are approaching the end of your 10 minutes – indicating that it is time to draw your presentation to a close.

You should note that overhead projectors and screens will not be available at the assessment centre. However, you can use a standalone laptop if the format is appropriate for an audience of three. My personal view is that laptops are not appropriate. The presentation is more of a 'sit opposite and talk you through' rather than a 'stand and present to a large audience using IT' type of situation. Before you call me old-fashioned, think about it: is a lot of technology really appropriate for a short presentation to three people in an 'office' type of situation?

After your presentation there is a 10-minute slot for questions on the presentation. The chairman may simply set the scene and then split the time 50/50 between the two panel members or may also wish to ask some questions and will allocate time to do this.

When the interview has been drawn to a close the panel will discuss your overall performance. They will consider whether your presentation should pass or be referred. A further series of criteria have been set to assess this and you will be expected to demonstrate:

- good oral communication
- presentation skills, i.e. eye contact, body language and voice projection
- clarity of thought, i.e. your presentation has a good structure

The above summarizes how the panel will operate and what they are looking for. I now want to give you some practical guidance in 10 simple steps concerning the presentation:

1 stage presence: all presentations involve a certain amount of acting/theatrics. Try to imagine you are on a stage giving a performance
2 preparation and rehearsal: prepare, plan and rehearse. Write your presentation out in full so that it can be read in around 13 to 14 minutes (you will not be reading verbatim on the day and will therefore naturally cut it down to around 10 minutes). Rehearse in front of colleagues, family and friends. Ensure that the first time you give your presentation is not at your final assessment. You've got plenty of time, make sure that you can deliver it backwards, standing on your head in 9 minutes and 59 seconds!

3   structure: think about the structure and break your presentation
     down into manageable chunks. Consider the following five Ps:
     ■ position: introduction – your name and outline of project, etc.
     ■ problem: key issues specific to the task
     ■ possibilities: lateral thought, options, why rejected, etc.
     ■ proposal: option adopted, critical appraisal, lessons learnt and
        closing remarks
     ■ preparation: forward plan and rehearse, rehearse, rehearse
     You will note that the above fits neatly in with the structure of
     the critical analysis. By following this structure you should
     achieve the 'clarity of thought' criterion that the panel is looking
     for
4   make it interesting: you only have 10 minutes so do not
     laboriously repeat the details of the property, its construction, etc.
     Get down to the problems and your solutions, i.e. the things that
     will interest the panel
5   the audience: it is important that you consider your audience.
     Think about how you will manage proceedings, the use of a short
     hand-out, etc.
6   key sentences: use sign posting at the beginning and end of each
     section of the presentation. For example, 'I would like to start by
     giving the panel a brief overview of my presentation' and, 'That
     concludes my opening remarks and I am now going to move on
     to ... key issues and problems that I was faced with'
7   pauses: don't race through the presentation at high speed. Think
     about your pace and use pauses to denote the natural breaks in
     the structure and to signify the next chunk or section of your text
8   visual aids: have a series of bullet points to jog your memory on a
     single sheet of paper or, if you need a little more, have the main
     headings with a series of bullet points on postcards which you
     can flick through during the presentation. You might also find a
     desktop flip chart useful
9   body language, voice and eye contact: whether you sit or stand
     may be dictated by the size of room and the distance between you
     and the panel. It is very off-putting if you choose to stand and

you are very close to the panel – you will give the impression of towering over them. If you are unable to stand well back, take the easy option and sit.

Think of how you use your voice in terms of volume, pace and tone to emphasize issues or changes in direction.

Eye contact is also important. If you are working from notes make sure that you keep looking up and making eye contact with the chairman. Every once in a while let your eye contact 'sweep' the other assessors

10 your appearance: don't forget to dress for success. Make sure that you feel confident as you walk through the door into the interview

QUESTIONING TECHNIQUE

Questioning technique is a key issue in any interview. It is the way in which the interviewer will gather the information to make a decision, based on the criteria, as to whether to employ, promote, dismiss or in our case pass the APC. It is important that you understand how the interviewer will operate and what techniques will be employed. Therefore in this section I have provided an insight into the various skills that will be employed by an interviewer.

During the course of the interview the assessors will mainly use open questions. An open question is where a sentence will start with the words: what, why, when, how, where or who. This technique will allow you to expand upon your answers and provide the information that is required to assess your competence.

There may be occasions when the interviewer will use closed questions. A closed question will elicit a yes/no or one word type of answer and will be used to clarify facts or information.

Assessors will ensure that questions are well phrased, unambiguous and concise. They will normally ask one question at a time and use short scenarios and narratives to help you understand the question. Supplementary questions will be used to probe and test your problem-solving ability and depth of knowledge. They may also be used to help and encourage you in moments of difficulty.

So far as practical guidance on questioning technique is concerned, you may find figure 11 useful.

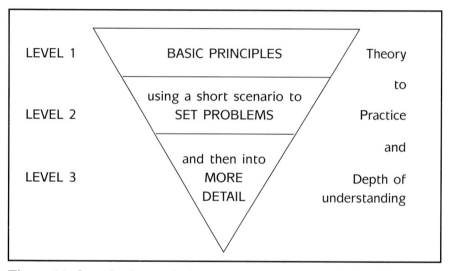

Figure 11 Questioning technique

The concept behind the inverted triangle is to signify the probing of depth of knowledge, skills and ability. Think in terms of three progressive levels of questioning:

■ level 1: tests basic principles or understanding of theory
■ level 2: tests your competence by setting an everyday practice problem to be resolved. This may be done by using a short scenario and then asking an open question. At this stage the assessors are also testing one of the main criteria for the assessment – your ability to put theory into practice
■ level 3: tests the full extent of your ability and knowledge by

adding to the breadth and complexity of the questioning or probing your lateral thinking. Have you thought about what you are doing, considered the advantages/disadvantages, options or why a particular methodology is used?

As an example of this questioning technique, the following is a typical line of questioning from the rural practice route. It is based on the agriculture and farm business management competency (Ref 001):

- 'In the area that you practice assume that you have been instructed to carry out a rental valuation. Please explain how you would go about the inspection, particularly in relation to the farm buildings, land and crops?' – level 1
- 'In preparing your rental valuation, what would you need to consider over and above the physical factors, such as budgeting and profitability? How would these matters affect your thinking and approach to the valuation?' – level 2
- 'Assume that you have completed your valuation and in so doing you discover that the tenant is trading at a loss. What factors would you consider or look at before advising him or her how to proceed with changing the business in terms of crops grown, overheads, marketing and general management?' – level 3

It is important to remember that in some of the optional competencies you have the choice to select levels. If competence is only required to level 1 or 2, the assessors' questioning does not probe beyond that point. But don't forget the final assessment is a part competency-based interview. Therefore, there are certain areas where you will be tested outside of your main areas of training and experience.

The above outlines the approach to questions relating to the core and optional competencies. You should also be aware of the approach that will be adopted to test the common competencies.

Your demonstration of ability in the common competencies will be woven into the main fabric of the interview. However, there will be times when you will face some specific questioning to gather evidence of competence. Some competencies such as law, mapping, measurement and the Rules of Conduct allow for very clearly-defined areas of questioning, and will often be linked to your core and optional competencies. On the other hand, personal and inter-personal skills will be demonstrated in your written reports and presentation, and also during the interview.

The panel will give careful thought to the depth of questioning on the common competencies. Guidance will be drawn from your training period and professional development record to give the assessors a feel for the level to which you can be questioned.

> Under the common competency of business skills you are required to understand quality control and assurance. You may have spent the last 12 months assisting your senior partner in setting up a complete quality management system within your firm or practice. Alternatively, you might have attended a two-hour training seminar. This sort of information will give the panel the guidance needed concerning questions on the common competencies.

Interviewee technique

I will now give you some practical guidance on how to be a good interviewee. Once again I have devised a simple 10-point guide:

1   ice breaker: make sure that you prepare for the ice breaker.

Give it some thought and use it to provide the panel with some further insight into your training and experience

2 pause for thought: before responding to questions always pause for thought. The panel will not be expecting you to leap into answers. Always stand back for a moment, consider the question, collect your thoughts and then deliver your response – look before you leap

3 active listening: think of listening in an interview as an active rather than a passive skill and make sure you concentrate on what is being said. In an exam you would read a question and then read it again. This will stimulate and recall information relevant to the subject/topic/issue. In an interview you will normally have only one chance, so practice repeating the words in your mind as the question is being asked by the assessor. This will help you commit the question to memory and assist your powers of recall when answering it

4 repeat the question: if you are not entirely sure what the question was, ask the assessor to repeat it. This is also a technique to employ if you get asked a long-winded and complicated question – it will force the assessor to re-visit the phrasing of the question and may help focus your thoughts. However, you should only do this sparingly

5 chronological order: think about your response in chronological order. A lot of questions that you will be asked will command a response which will naturally have a chronological order: anything to do with the techniques employed or the order of carrying out or performing a particular task or function. This will help you collect your thoughts and ensure that you do not miss any important aspects of the response required

6 key issues: if there is no chronological order you may think of your response in terms of key issues or bullet points. You may find it helpful to use the various competency standards as a guide to your preparation for the interview. These statements will provide the trigger for the areas of questioning by the panel and may help you focus whilst preparing for the interview

7   unfamiliar areas of experience: you will be asked questions where you are outside of your main areas of experience. In these instances do not be frightened to qualify your response. Don't forget, the assessor may have put you outside your main areas of experience to test how well you can draw from them and apply this learning and knowledge to an unfamiliar territory. Make sure you qualify your answers in terms of whether you have limited or no experience in any particular subject area

8   mental blocks: everyone suffers from nerves during an interview situation. There may be occasions when you have a complete mental block or you may stumble with the answer. Don't worry, the panel will not expect you to answer every question. You will also be offered the opportunity to come back on areas of questioning at the end of the interview

9   bluffing: don't try to bluff or waffle your way through any of the answers. The assessors are all very experienced surveyors and will probably detect when you are unsure or are attempting to guess the answers. This will also give a bad impression in terms of duty of care and being aware of your limitations. Often when we are unsure in an interview our body language or tone of voice can be a give away. If you are not sure of an issue or really have no idea of the response required simply tell the panel. Do not worry if you come across one or two questions that you are unable to answer, the panel will not expect you to answer everything

10   final word: you will be offered the last word by the chairman when the interview is drawing to a close. At this stage only re-open an area of questioning if it is absolutely vital. Close the interview by thanking the assessors for their time, smile and leave the room

NOTE TAKING

The assessors will take brief notes during the interview. In keeping a record of the interview, assessors will ensure that they are being fair to candidates. Also where appropriate, this will assist in the preparation of referral reports. So do not be put off or unnerved if you see the panel writing a few notes. This is being done for your benefit to ensure that the final assessment is a fair and impartial assessment of your performance.

EQUAL OPPORTUNITIES

The need to be conscious of equal opportunities will crop up in many aspects of the final assessment process. The following is a summary of the main issues:

- the assessors will keep a record of the interview
- the chairman will handle the opening five minutes with great care to help settle your nerves
- the chairmen will ensure that you are 'fit and well and ready to proceed'. He or she will check that you are not suffering from ill health
- the chairman should control time across the interview as a whole and within the various components
- the assessors will link questions to your training and experience in terms of the common, core and optional competencies
- questioning will mainly relate to the criteria set down for the APC
- the chairman will give you the last word before drawing the interview to a close

CONDUCT, BEST PRACTICE AND CUSTOMER CARE

The panel will think of you as their customer and consider 'best practice' to be about the delivery of excellent customer care. The preparation beforehand, the tone of voice when asking questions and the way that the assessors look at you during the interview will all affect how you feel and, therefore, perform.

In an interview situation, these matters are important to both the interviewer and interviewee. Let us now consider some of these issues from both sides of the interview table:

■ room layout: the chairman will ensure the environment within which the interview will take place is prepared for you (i.e. you won't be staring into the sun). He or she will check that the panel have name cards in front of them so that you are not forced to try and remember names from the introductions. Before you enter the room think about how you will greet the panel. As soon as you enter the room decide where you will put your plans, papers, etc.

■ eye contact: you must always remain attentive and appear interested. However, do not spend the whole time 'eyeballing' the chairman or one of the assessors. Try to think about looking just over the interviewers' left shoulder, right shoulder or to the chest. This will take the sting out of the eye contact but will still signal to the panel that you are focused and attentive

■ 60 minutes is a long time to remain attentive. It is easy to gaze out of the window for a few minutes, read from some of the details you have in front of you or fidget. Stay conscious of the impact that such actions may have on the panel

■ body language: you must be aware of the impact that body language can have on your performance. You must be conscious of your facial expressions: a pained look may immediately convey the impression that you are finding an area of questioning difficult. Never underestimate the importance of a smile in terms of building a rapport with the panel. Also think about how you sit. Avoid sitting with your arms crossed, or leaning forward, eyeball to eyeball, and speaking in a harsh or agitated tone of voice! This will not give the panel a good opinion of you

■ voice projection: your tone needs to be warm and enthusing, the volume positive and confident and the pace should be such that the panel are able to follow and understand your answers

■ listening skills: your ability to listen and concentrate during the course of an interview is important for two reasons. First, to ensure that you interpret the interviewer's questions correctly; and secondly, to help you convey interest and attention through positive body language

■ closing the interview: before drawing the interview to a close, the chairman will ask if you have anything else to say. This opportunity will be kept within the parameters of the interview. The chairman might say, 'Is there anything that we have discussed that you would like to add to or clarify?' – in using these words the chairman will avoid re-opening the interview. The chairman will then probably say, 'The interview is now finished. Thank you for attending'. He or she will stand, perhaps a final shake of the hands, and gesture or lead you to the door. It is important that you leave on a positive note, so try to smile and don't forget to say thank you.

SUMMARY

■ An interview is an information-gathering process, the aim being to provide the interviewer with the information that will satisfy the criteria for the interview.

■ Rehearse your opening lines so that you get off to a good start. This will help with your nerves.

■ Dress for success. If you look good, you will also feel good.

■ If you are unwell, advise the RICS staff at the assessment centre and they will provide you with any assistance required.

■ Practice your presentation extensively before the day so that you can deliver it with confidence.

■ In discussion with your supervisor, counsellor or colleagues, try and anticipate the questions that may be asked on your presentation.

■ Focus on the criteria that have been set for your presentation: good oral communication skills, presentation skills and clarity of thought.

■ Understand the difference between open and closed questions and practice responses in a chronological order or by summarizing key points.

■ Practice active listening.

■ Use the competency statements whilst preparing and revising for the interview. These statements will act as the focal point for the questions from the panel.

■ Do not be put off by the panel taking notes. This is for your benefit to ensure that the final assessment is fair and is based upon the evidence presented by you.

■ At the end of the interview always smile and thank the panel for their time.

6 Appraisal, referral and the appeal system

This chapter will consider what happens after the final assessment interview. It will look at how the assessment panel reach their decision, referral reports and how you can make an appeal.

CANDIDATE APPRAISAL

Before the final assessment interview commenced, the chairman will have agreed with the panel that there should be four to five minutes of silence after you leave the room. This period of quiet reflection allows panel members to review notes, events, answers and to start evaluating performance generally, so that a balanced appraisal may be reached. A large part of this process will involve the panel members considering how the details of your training and experience have stood up to questioning during the interview. As a starting point, they will consider your performance against the five broad headings that equate to the concept of 'competent to practise' (see chapter 1). The assessors will be linking the common, core and optional competencies to these five headings to arrive at their decision. Although there is a great deal of overlap, for example you will demonstrate your oral communication skills every time you answer a question, in any of the competencies the mental links the assessors will make are set out in figure 12.

It is vital therefore that you have a clear picture in your mind of what being 'competent to practise' looks like from the outset. Your

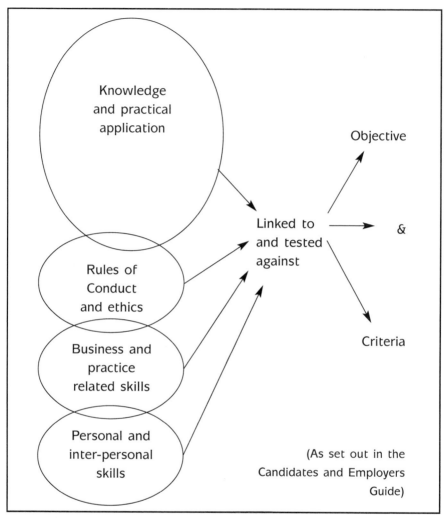

Figure 12 Candidate appraisal

goal should be to demonstrate these five areas of skill and ability during your final assessment interview.

As well as questioning you on your training and experience, the panel will check to ensure that you meet with the minimum training requirement of 400 days of experience within 24 calendar months.

The panel will then move on and consider your critical analysis and presentation. These will be considered against the criteria that had been set for these components of the final assessment (see chapters 4 and 5). Finally, they will consider your interim and final assessment records. They will also check that your professional development meets with the minimum requirement of 48 hours per annum.

DRAWING THE SIX COMPONENTS TOGETHER – THE HOLISTIC VIEW

The panel will draw the six components of the final assessment together on the front page of the marking form as shown in figure 13. There are three columns on the form: refer, marginal and pass. This allows the panel to take a holistic view of your performance and then make the decision as to whether you are considered 'competent to practise'. Therefore, no one element of the assessment will constitute a pass or a referral. All candidates are different and skills will vary. Some candidates will show strength in technical and professional matters and perhaps be a little weaker with inter-personal and communication skills. With other candidates, the opposite may apply. The panel will take an overall view of your performance. However, if any of the six components fall so far short of the criteria that the refer box is ticked, you will be referred over all and will have to re-take the whole assessment.

Role of the chairman

During this decision-making period, the chairman will ensure that the forms are completed as a consensus of opinion, representing the panel's final view. He or she will listen to the panel members, particularly with regard to their areas of specialism, and will weigh and balance the view of the panel to ensure that the final decision is fair.

THE ROYAL INSTITUTION OF CHARTERED SURVEYORS

Affix Photo Here

ASSESSMENT OF PROFESSIONAL COMPETENCE

SPRING/AUTUMN ....

Name of Candidate ....

Number .... Age ....

Firm's Name ....

Previously Referred   YES/NO

Specialist Area ....

I commenced the APC before January 1997   YES/NO   (delete as applicable)

FOR OFFICE USE ONLY - PLEASE DO NOT WRITE BELOW THIS LINE

Currently recording   Experience route ☐ (1 year monitored experience)

☐   Diary exempt ☐ (No diary required)

                             Mature Entry ☐ (1 year monitored experience)

                             Special consideration _____

FINAL ASSESSMENT

Overall Assessment	Refer	Marginal	Pass
Training and Experience			
Interim and Final Assessment Records			
Professional Development			
Critical Analysis			
Record of Progress			
Presentation			
Interview			

Overall Result: **REFER/PASS**   (delete as necessary)

Chairman (Block Capitals) ....

Signature ....   Date ....

Assessor ....   Assessor ....

Figure 13 Marking form

THE FINAL DECISION

It should be remembered that you will not be expected to demonstrate the level of knowledge and experience equivalent to that of an experienced practitioner. The panel's decision will be based on you having demonstrated competence to the required level tested against the various criteria that have been set. The panel will not be expecting a level of knowledge equal to that of their advanced years!

It is also worth noting that there are no quotas or pass rates for the APC. The bench-marks that the assessment panel will be working to are the levels of competence required in the *APC Requirements and Competencies* tested against the various criteria that have been set out in the *Candidates and Employers Guide*. All candidates that meet with these requirements will pass the final assessment.

REFERRAL REPORTS

Results will be sent to you by first-class post within 21 days from the date of your interview. Remember to let the RICS know if your correspondence address changes. A pass list will also be published on the RICS website after each assessment period. However, for security reasons no results will be given over the telephone, by fax or to a third party.

In the event of a referral, the chairman of your assessment panel will provide as much information as possible to you. The referral report will be linked to the six components of the final assessment; the training period; interim and final assessment records; professional development; critical analysis; presentation; and interview. The panel will have been asked to give reasons why you have not met the required levels of competence. This should be with reference to the specific competency and with a clear explanation of how you have fallen short of the criteria. You may also receive advice on further training and development that has been identified by the panel.

Finally, you may receive feedback on aspects of your performance that were satisfactory. The objective of this is to enable you to address these weaknesses before the next assessment in six month's time and be successful when you re-sit.

The receipt of a referral report will be a miserable experience. However, you must remain positive and focused. Go back to some of the key concepts behind the critical analysis, be introspective, learn from your mistakes and improve areas of weakness. You have had the benefit of the experience, learn from it and build upon your strengths so that you are successful on the next occasion. Be philosophical. It may be that you were not quite ready for the final assessment.

If you are referred, there are some minimum requirements that you must satisfy before you re-sit the final assessment:

- record a minimum of a further 100 days relevant professional experience. The assessors will probably give you guidance on this
- undertake a minimum of a further 24 hours professional development
- write a new critical analysis; or if recommended, re-submit the original, suitably amended and updated
- complete a summary forward plan to cover the further 100 days of training and experience. After this you will complete a summary of progress form. Another supervisor's and counsellor's report form will also need to be completed. All of these forms can be found at the back of the *Candidates and Employers Guide*
- you will need to submit a copy of your record of progress giving details of the further 100 days of training and experience in relation to the competencies
- be re-interviewed and give a presentation on the relevant critical analysis

APPEALS

If you are unsuccessful and you are in any way aggrieved by any aspect of the final assessment, you can make an appeal. This must be received by the RICS no later than 14 days from your result being posted to you. The details of how and when to lodge an appeal will be sent with the referral report and application for reassessment.

If you do feel aggrieved, my advice is as follows:

- it is very difficult to get a feel for the outcome of an interview immediately afterwards. Your nerves and adrenaline will still be high and you will find it difficult to be truly objective
- if you are feeling aggrieved as soon as you get home, sit down and write a list of the aspects of the interview that went well and then make a list of the aspects that didn't go well and why you are feeling unhappy
- give it 24 hours and then go back to your notes and consider whether there were any aspects you still consider to be unfair

When you receive the result you may be pleasantly surprised. I remember receiving telephone calls from two candidates immediately after their assessments claiming it was unfair and wanting guidance on how to appeal. Shortly afterwards they received their results and both rang me to say, rather sheepishly, that they had passed. Therefore, don't react to one or two aspects of the assessment that did not go so well. The tendency in a highly-charged interview situation is to only remember the downsides.

In my view, there are three main reasons why an appeal might be validly made:

1 administrative or procedural matters: the panel may not have been provided with the correct information and detail or something has gone wrong, for example you have not been given the opportunity of making your presentation

2 questioning and testing of competence that has concentrated too much outside of your main areas of training and experience
3 any form of discrimination

Hopefully such problems will not arise and in my experience it is often your perception of events that will colour your judgement, rather than what actually happened. However, it is for this reason that the RICS has established an appeal system.

THE APPEAL SYSTEM

If you do want to make an appeal it is important that it is made by you and not a third party. You must clearly state the grounds upon which your appeal is made and provide the necessary supporting evidence.

After some additional research has been carried out by the RICS, your appeal will be considered by the chairman of the Practice Qualification Group and two nominated members from the faculty of your chosen route.

If your appeal is successful, your fee will be returned and a reassessment, using all of the original paperwork, will be arranged as soon as possible. You will be reassessed by a different panel and the normal rules and procedures will apply. Alternatively, your appeal will be rejected and you will be eligible for reassessment along the lines of the notification that was sent to you with your referral report.

SEEKING ADVICE AND FURTHER GUIDANCE

▪ be introspective and do some soul searching. Is there anything you can learn from a referral to make you successful on the next occasion?
▪ with your referral report at hand talk to your employer and your supervisor and counsellor

- you might also wish to approach your regional training adviser, APC doctor or the RICS
- consider how additional professional development may assist you with addressing any shortcomings in your referral report

SUMMARY

- Ensure that your paperwork and final submissions are in order. The panel will be checking to ensure that you meet the training and experience requirements (i.e. 400 days minimum within 24 calendar months) and the final assessment record and professional development requirements.
- In drawing the six components of the final assessment together (i.e. training and experience; interim and final assessment records; professional development; critical analysis; presentation; and interview) the panel will take a holistic view of your performance.
- The decision will be arrived at by considering the views and opinions of all three panel members. This is to ensure a fair and balanced outcome.
- The six components of the final assessment will be weighted but all the assessment criteria must be met.
- The panel will not be working to quotas or pass rates.
- If you are unhappy with the interview and wish to make an appeal try and be objective. Seek advice from your supervisor and counsellor.
- If you do make an appeal it must be no later than 14 days from your result being posted to you.

Conclusion

I would like to conclude this book by reiterating some of the comments I made in chapter 1. The APC is first and foremost a period of training and practical experience. If you follow the guidance and ensure that you are learning the skills and reaching the levels of attainment required in the various competencies, you will be well on your way to a successful final assessment interview. If the training and experience has been correctly put in place over the two-year period leading up to the final assessment, the outcome should be a formality.

It is when candidates have not followed the various guidance that is available and have not remained focused on the competency requirements that the final assessment results in an unsatisfactory outcome.

It is also essential that you focus on the various skills required for the final assessment: report writing; presentation; and interview skills. The practical guidance set out in the previous chapters will provide you with some insight to the challenge that lies ahead, not just the APC but also the rest of your career.

The following is a list of the common pitfalls and problems that you should avoid at all costs:

- you cannot start recording experience until the RICS has accepted your application for enrolment
- if you change employer during the training period you must inform the RICS
- the training period is a minimum of 400 days within 24 calendar months
- professional development is a minimum of 48 hours per annum
- the interim assessment must be completed within one month of the first 12 months and you must then complete a further 12 months of training and experience before you are eligible for the final assessment
- you must record the number of competencies and to the levels required by your route before you are eligible for the final assessment
- the final assessment is a part competency-based interview so be ready for those questions that are outside of your main areas of training and experience. Remember, you are being interviewed to test whether you are 'competent to practise' as a chartered surveyor
- don't forget your supervisor and counsellor declarations on the:
    - training agreement
    - competency achievement planner
    - diary
    - log book
    - record of progress
    - interim and final assessment records
    - critical analysis
- stay focused on the competency statements for your route and particularly the criteria that overarch the assessment and apply specifically to the critical analysis and presentation
- and finally, you have 14 days from the date that your results are posted by the RICS in which to make an appeal

I would like to offer you one final thought based upon my 25-years' experience as a chartered surveyor, and that is your APC never ends.

Your professional competence will continue to be assessed by employers, clients and peer groups throughout your career. It is uncertainty that creates the need for experts and, as the world around you changes in terms of consumer demands, law and technology, the content and focus of your training and development will change. When you become chartered think of the Institution's programme of CPD as a vehicle to assist you with these never-ending training and development needs.

Index

acknowledgement of application 8, 22
advice *see* guidance
agreement *see* structured training
APC doctors 10
APC helpline 9
APC Requirements and Competencies 1, 5, 8, 16, 32, 79
appeals 9, 81–2
  procedure 82
  reasons for 81–2
application
  for enrolment 7–8, 22
  for final assessment 38–9
appraisal of candidate 75–7
assessment *see* final assessment; interim assessment
assessment criteria
  developmental 42–3
  immediate 42
assessment panel 2, 41, 46
  candidate appraisal 75–7
  chairman's role 35, 57–60, 77
  decision 46, 63, 79
  equal opportunities 71
  interviewing technique 65–70
  note taking 70–1

best practice 71–3
body language, candidate 72–3
brainstorming 53
business skills 18, 68

candidate
  appearance 60–1, 65
  appraisal 75–7
  body language 72–3
  conduct and best practice 71–3
  interview technique 68–70
  listening skills 69, 72–3
  preparation for interview 60–1, 63–5
  reports on 35–6, 48–9
  self-appraisal 52
Candidates and Employers Guide 1, 8
  APC objective 41
  assessment criteria 42
  certification of work 52
  critical analysis (report) 50, 51
  interim assessment forms 36
  professional development guidance 20
  re-sit requirements 80
  record of progress 6, 32–3
Candidates Structured Training Framework 24
certification, critical analysis 52
chairman, assessment panel 35, 57–60, 77
change of employer 7, 22, 29–30
chartered surveyor 33, 41
common competencies 7, 18–19
  questions 68
competence to practise 4–5, 41, 44, 75–6, 77
competencies 15–19
  building pathology example 16–17
  common 5, 17, 18–19, 68
  core 17, 19
  final assessment 19, 43–8

Index

competencies – *contd.*
  full list 16
  levels 16–18
  optional 17, 19, 67
  record of progress 32–3
  reference number 32
competencies table 24
competency achievement planner 5–6, 21, 22, 24–6
  example 25
compulsory competencies 18
conduct of candidate 71–3
Continuing Professional Development (CPD) 7
core competencies 17, 19
  questions 68
counsellor 8
  certification of work 52
  employer as 12
  report on candidate 35–6, 48
  responsibilities 33–4
CPD *see* Continuing Professional Development
criteria, final assessment interview 41–3, 44–6
critical analysis (report) 49–55
  certification 52
  critical (self) appraisal 52
  format 50
  key issues 50–1, 54
  options and solutions 51
  presentation 62–5
  report writing guidance 52–5
customer care 71–3

dates 7–9, 85
  acknowledgement of application 8
  appeal 9, 81
  attainment levels 17–18
  diary (commencement) 29
  enrolment 7–8, 22
  final assessment 9, 22, 35, 38, 39
  interim assessment 9, 35
  results 9, 79
  reviews 8, 34
deadlines 7–9
  see also dates

definition of APC 2
diary 2, 6, 29–30
  format 29
documents 5–6, 7
  checklist 39

employer
  agreement 23–4
  change of 7, 22, 29–30
  role of 10–13
enrolment 7–8, 22–3
  acknowledgement of 29
equal opportunities 71

faculties 2, 15
final assessment 38–55
  appeals 81–2
  critical analysis 49–55
  date 9, 22, 35, 38, 39
  paperwork 38–9
  record 48–9
  re-sit requirements 80
  reassessment 82
  referral reports 79–80
  results 79
  streamlined approach 4–5
final assessment interview 2, 40–8, 56–74
  candidate's role 60–1
  chairman's role 35, 57–60, 77
  competencies 43–8
  criteria 41–3, 44–6
  decision of panel 46, 63, 79
  holistic view 4, 77–8
  ice breaker 59, 68–9
  objective 41
  part-competency based 19, 43–4, 47, 67
  preparation and revision 40, 46–8, 63–5
  presentation 62–5
  questioning technique 65–70
  questions 41, 44–6, 54
  stress management 58–60
  structure of 59, 61–2
final assessment record 48–9
forms
  application 8, 22

final assessment 39
  interim assessment 35–6
  see also record keeping; tables

guidance 85
  presentation 63–5
  referral 82–3
  training agreement 23–4
guides to APC 1

help 9–10
  see also guidance
helpline 9

information management 28–37
information technology 18
interim assessment 35–7
  date 9
  format 36–7
  forms 35–6
interview *see* final assessment interview
interviewing technique
  assessment panel 65–70
  candidate 68–70

key concepts 4–7
key dates *see* dates
key documents 5–6, 7

law 18, 68
log book 2, 6, 31
  format 31

management skills 42
mapping 18, 68
measurement 18, 68
membership of RICS 2–3
  route to 3
monitoring table 24, 26

optional competencies 17, 19
  questions 67

part-competency based interview 19, 43–4, 47, 67
personal and interpersonal skills 18, 68

pitfalls of assessment 85
planning
  professional development 20
  training 35–6, 48
Practice Qualification Group 4
presentation at interview 62–5
  guidance on 63–5
  rehearsal 63
  structure 64
  visual aids 64
professional competence 4–5
professional development 2, 6–7, 19–21, 31–2, 36
  annual plan 20
  interim assessment 36
progress, record of 6, 32–3
progress reports 33–5
project report *see* critical analysis

questioning technique
  assessment panel 65–8
  example 67
  interviewee 68–70
  levels of questioning 66–7
  types of questions 41, 45–6, 54

re-sit requirements 80
record keeping 28–37
  diary 29–30
  log book 31
  professional development 31–2
progress reports 33–5
  record of progress 2, 6, 32–3
record of progress 2, 6, 32–3
  format 32
referral reports 79–80
  guidance on 82–3
regional training advisors 10, 35
rehearsal, presentation 63
report writing 52–5
reports *see* critical analysis; progress reports
results 9, 79
reviews
  six-monthly 8, 32–3
  three-monthly 8, 32–3

Index

RICS website 10
Rules of Conduct 23, 44, 45, 46, 47, 68

self-assessment 37
six-monthly reviews 8, 32–3
skills *see* competencies
stress management, final interview 58–60
structure
  final interview 59, 61–2
  presentation 64
structured training 2, 3, 5–6, 21–6
  agreement 5, 21, 22, 23–4
  competency achievement planner 21, 22,
    24–6
  timing of 21–3
substitution, competencies 16
supervisor 8
  employer as 12
  report on candidate 35–6, 48

responsibilities 33–4
Supervisors and Counsellors Guide 33

tables 24, 26
three-monthly reviews 8, 32–3
timing *see* dates
training 15–26
  agreement 23–4
  competency achievement planner 24–6
  employer's role 11
  planning 35–6, 48
  regional training advisors 10, 35
  see also structured training

visual aids
  critical analysis 50, 53
  presentation 64

website 10